Carrie Osburn Designs Presents

DOODLEDALA IV

by Carrie Osburn

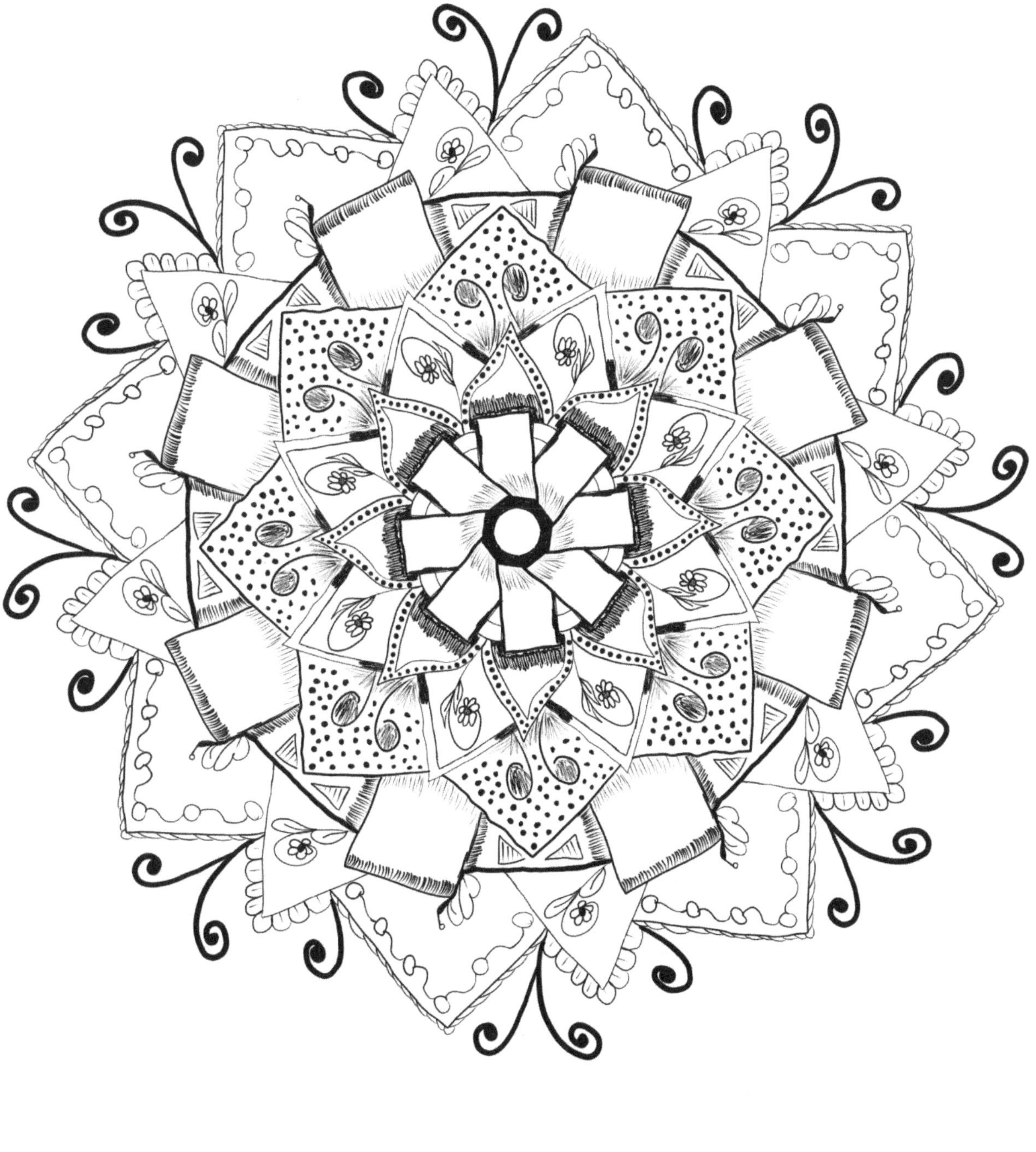

Copyright

This book is Dedicated too

To those following their dreams...
Just because you aren't making progress as fast
as you think you should does not mean
you aren't making progress.
Keep going.

A Special Thanks to my Patreons

Renata Page
Cindy Nation
Tamara Slaten

Find Me on the Web

carrieosburndesigns.com
facebook.com/carrieosburndesigns
facebook.com/groups/carrieosburndesigns

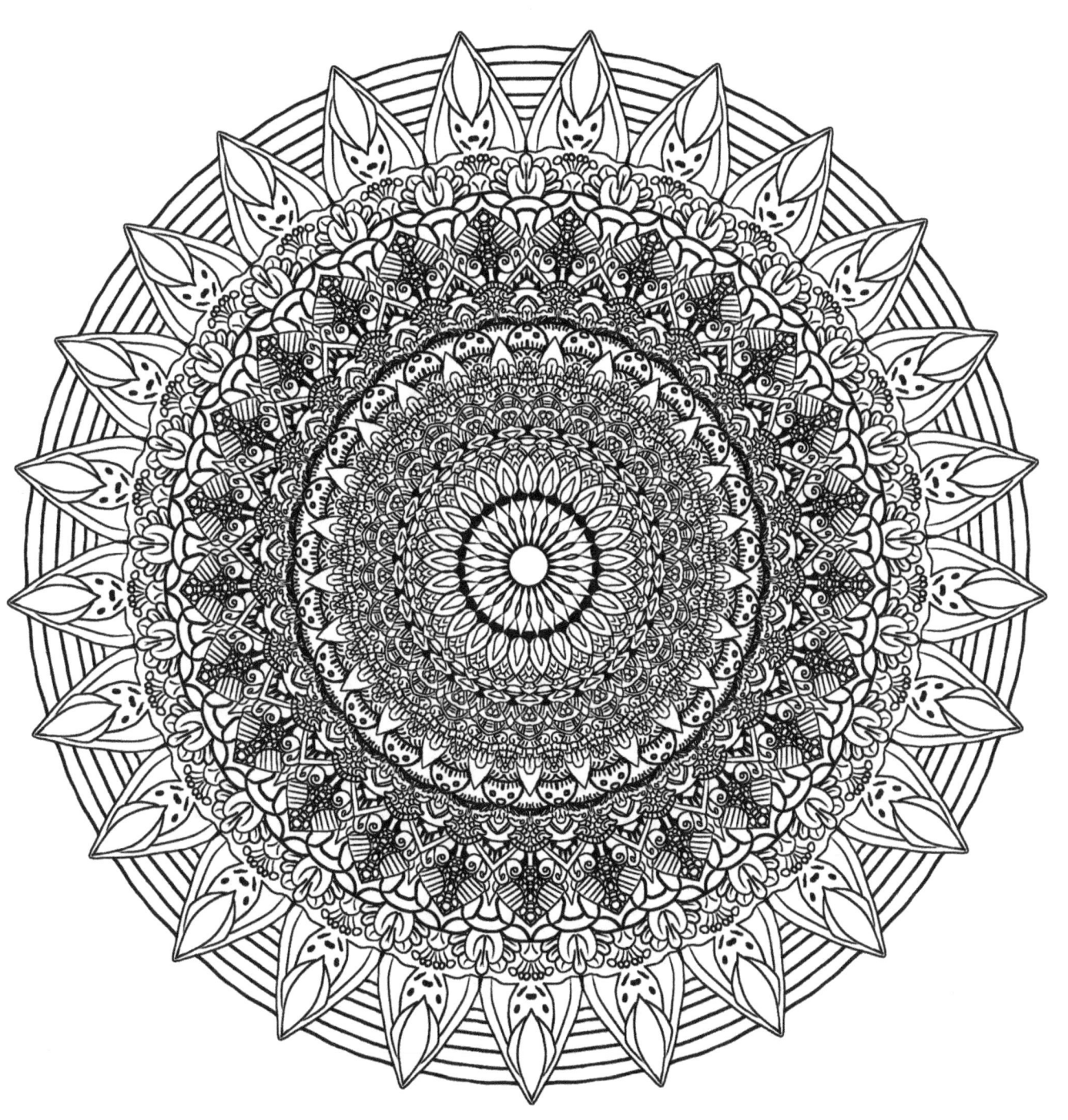

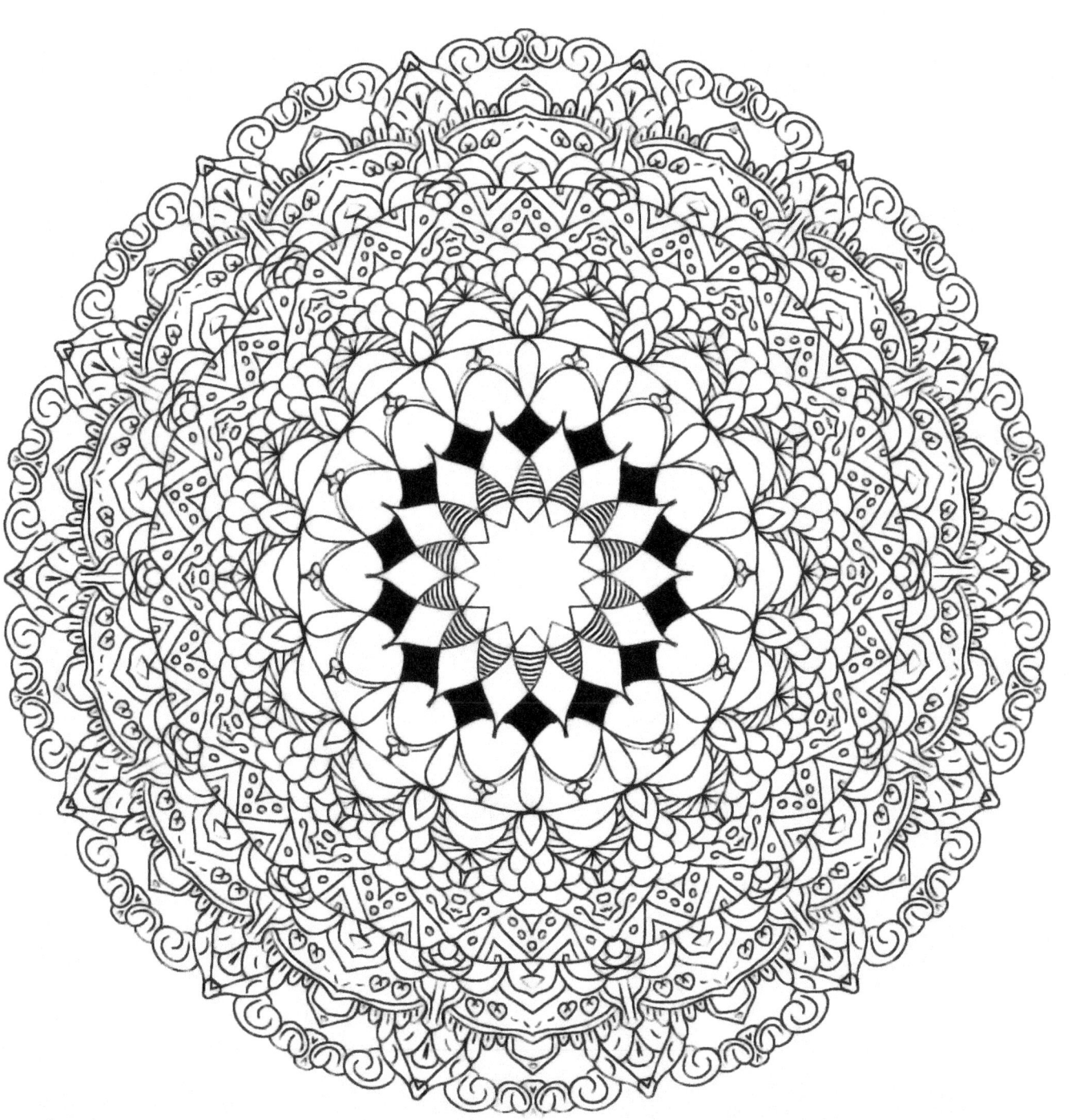

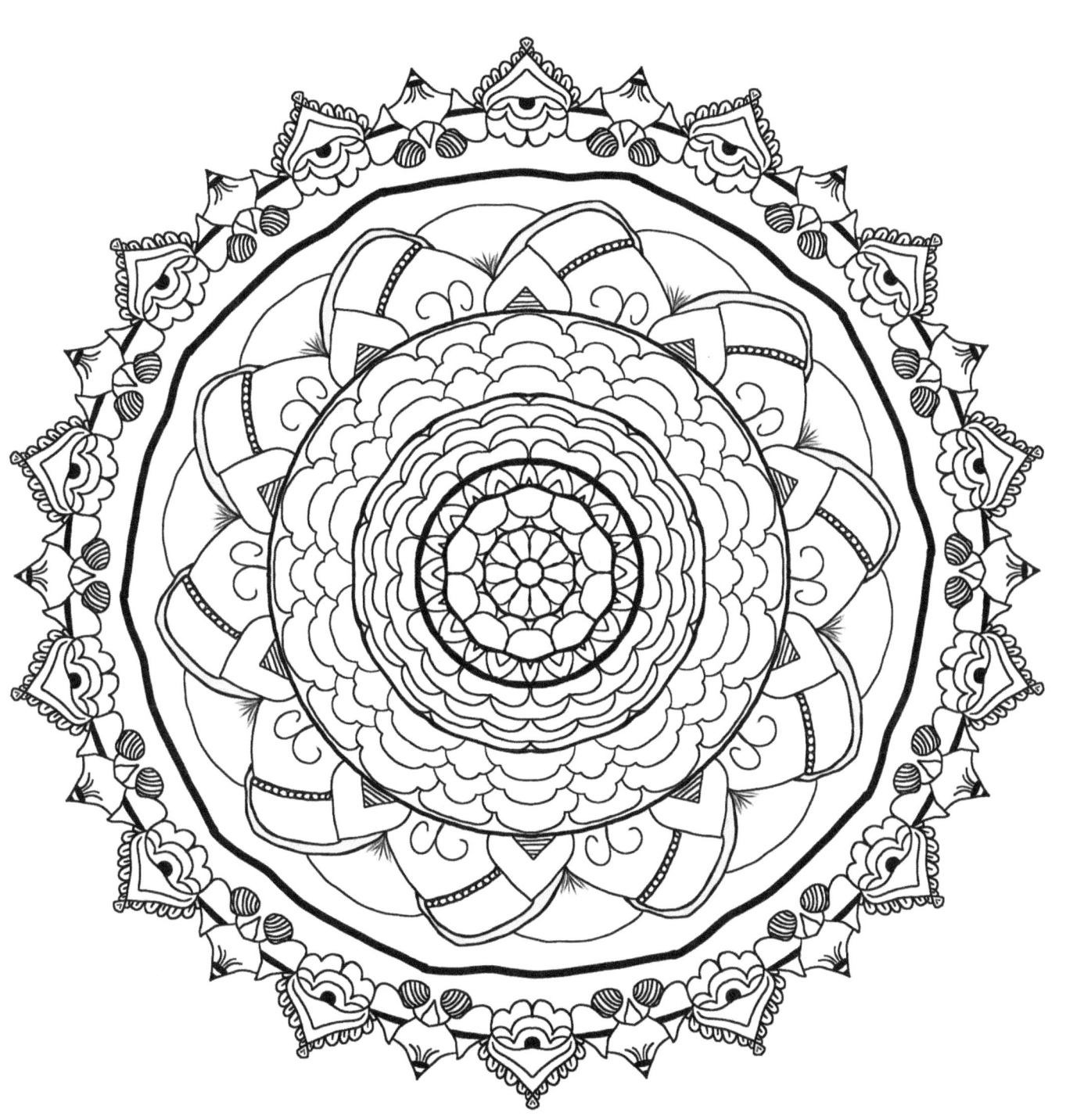

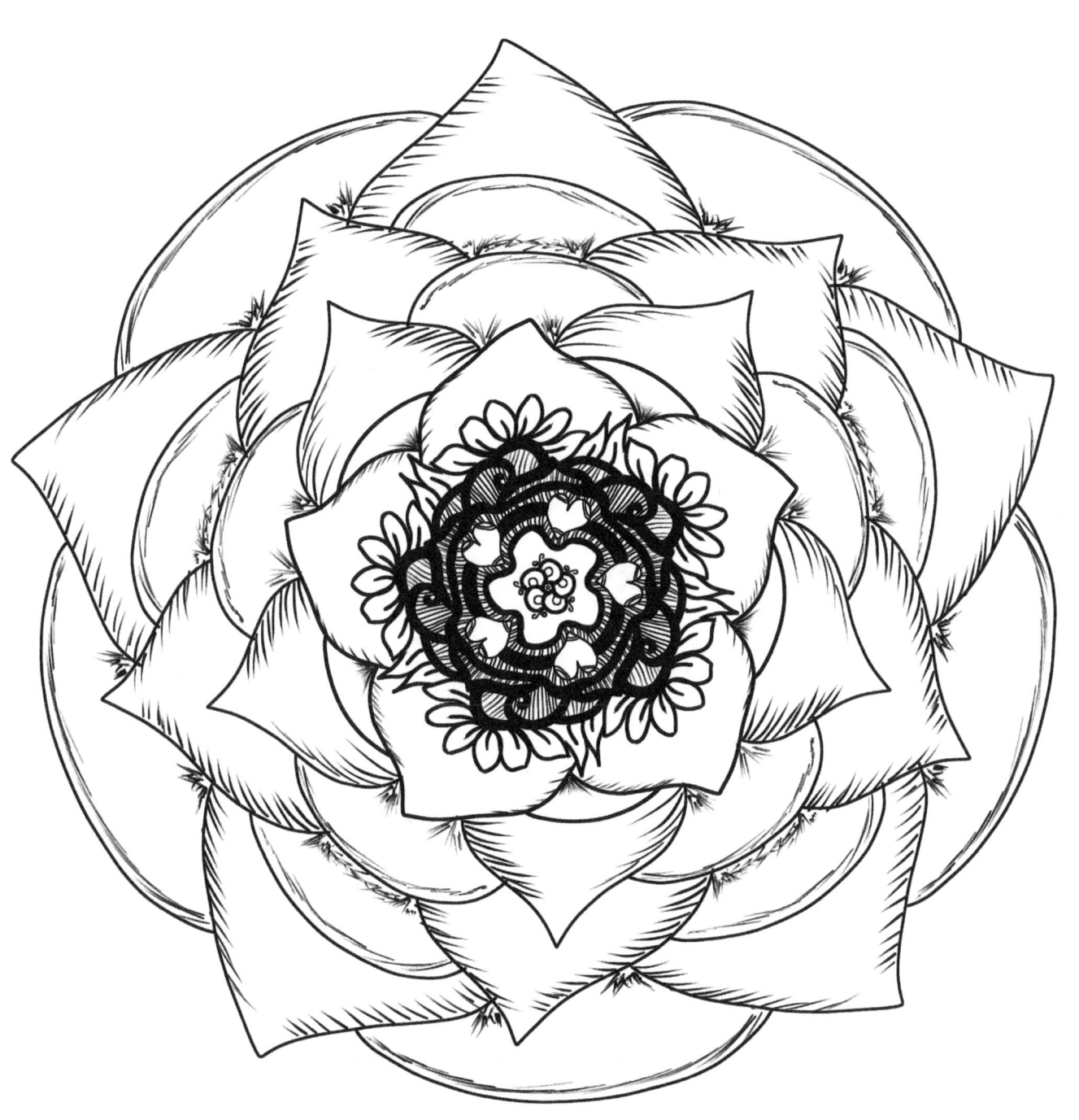

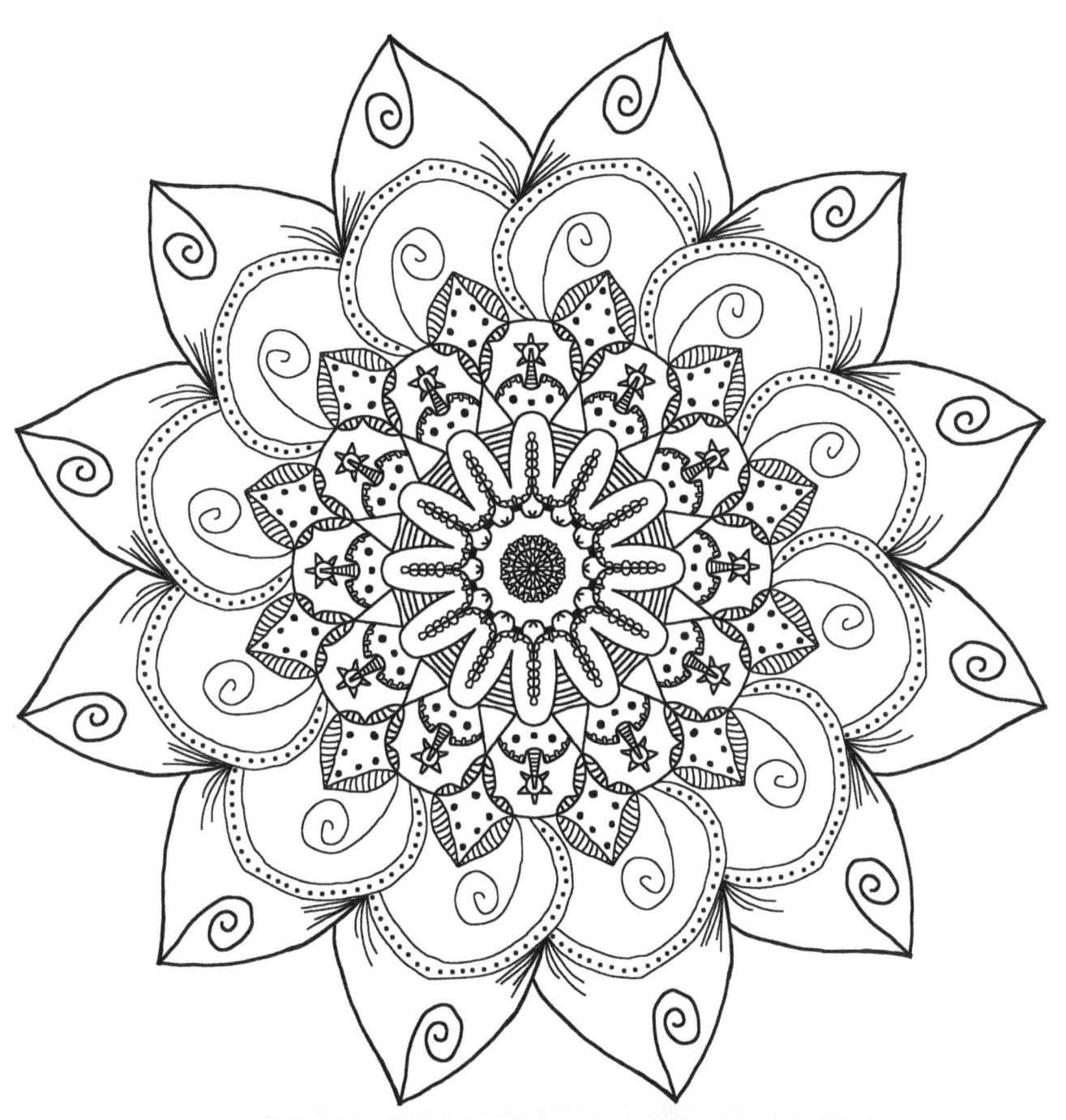

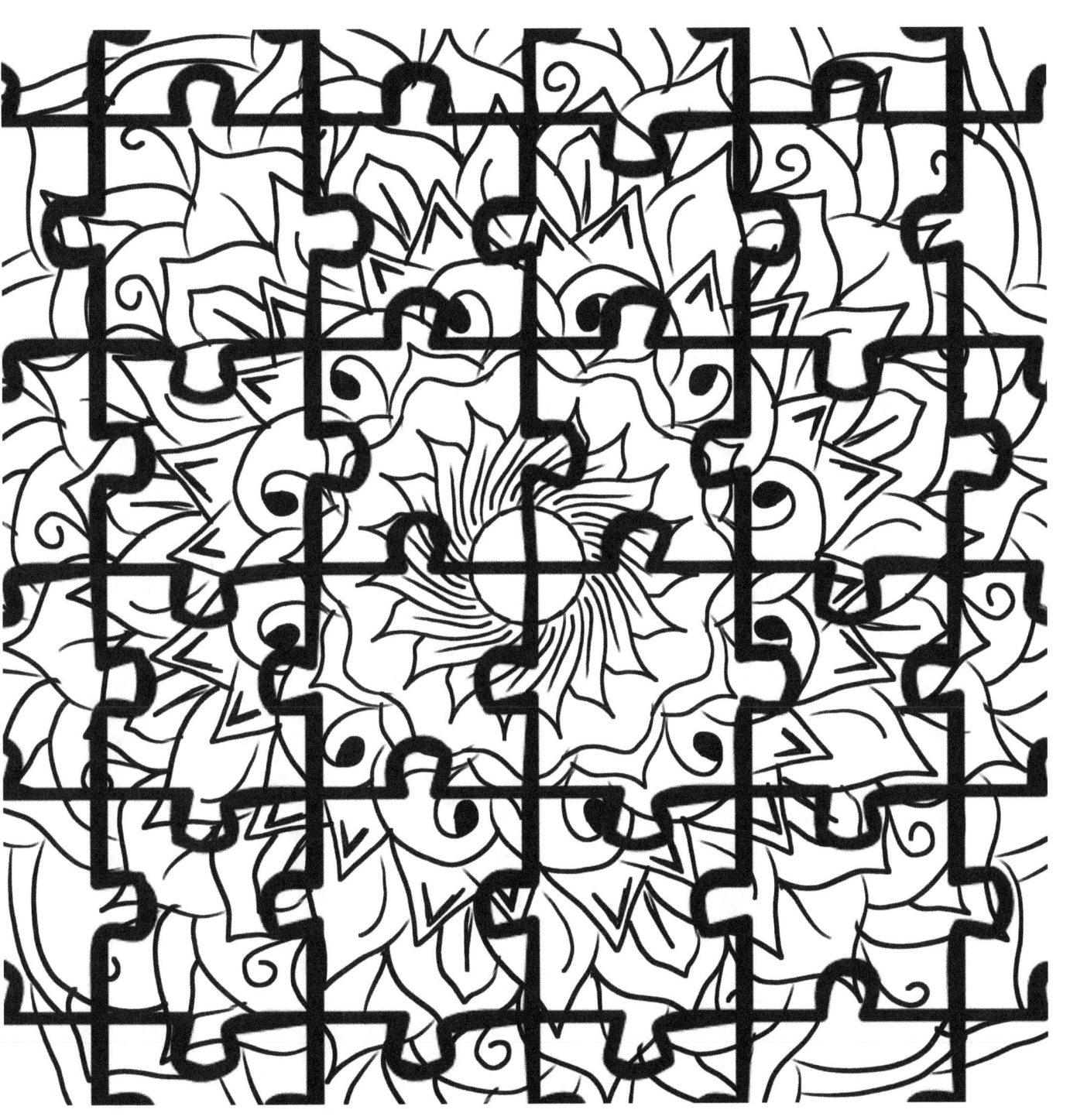

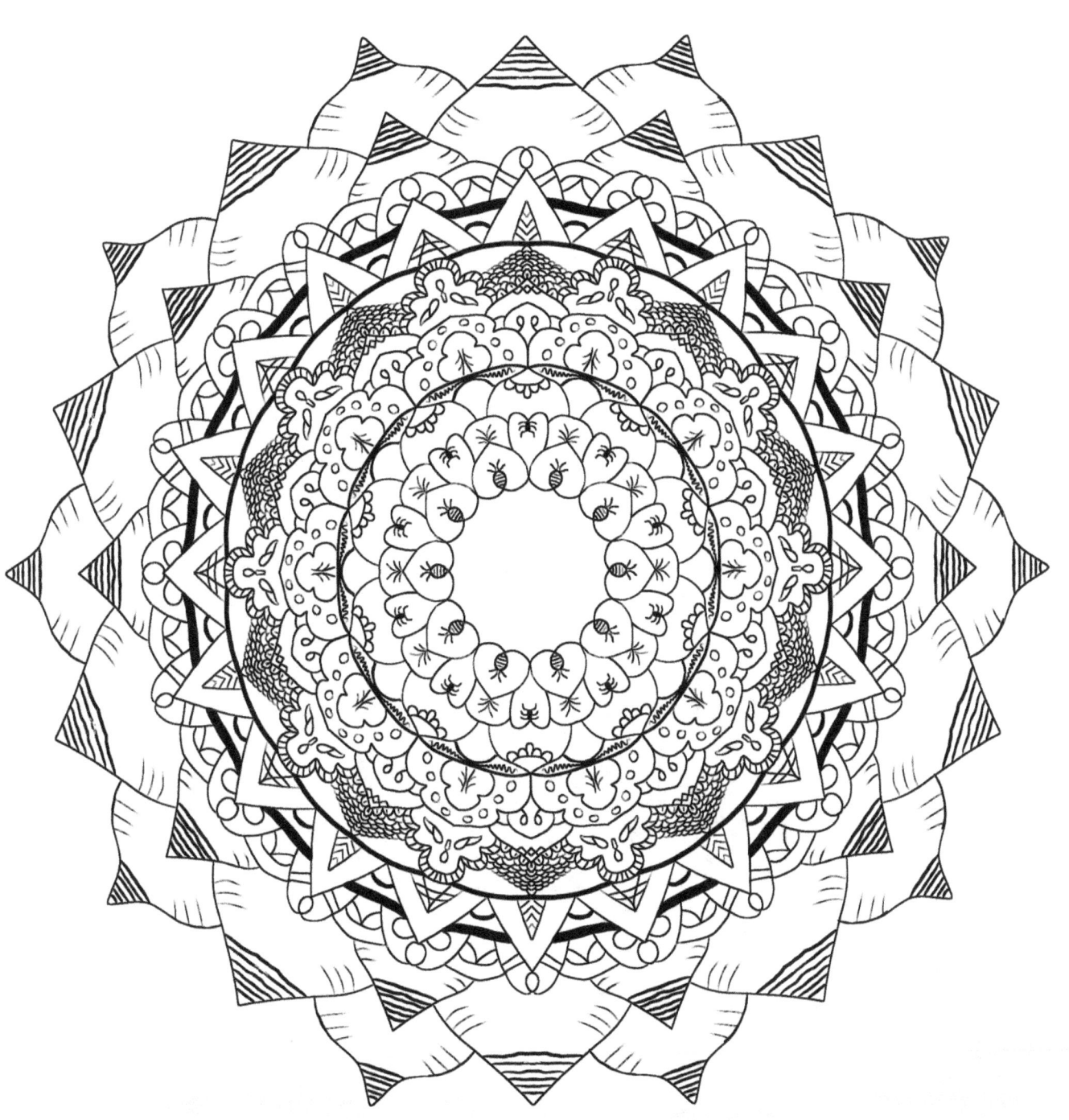

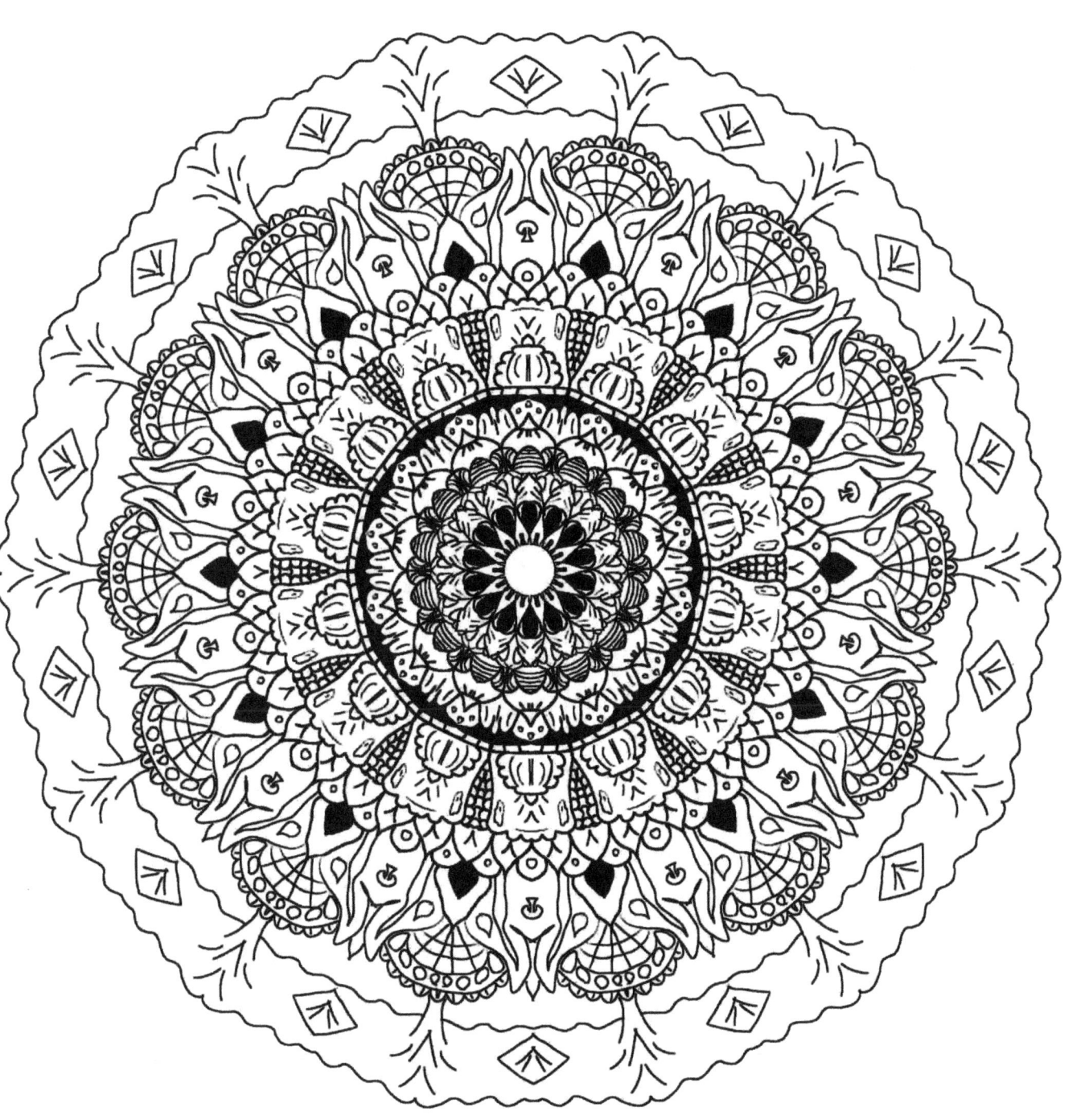

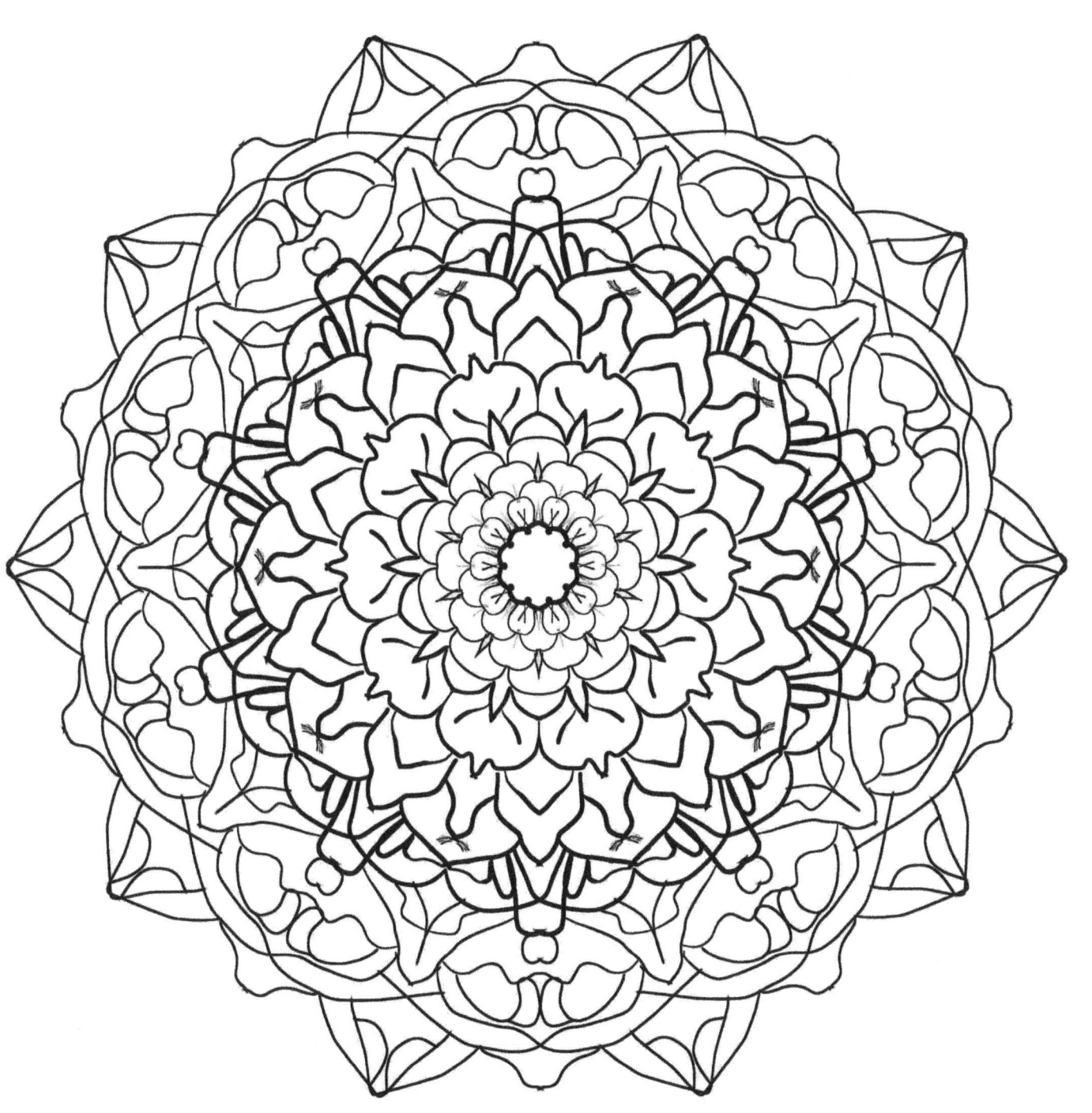

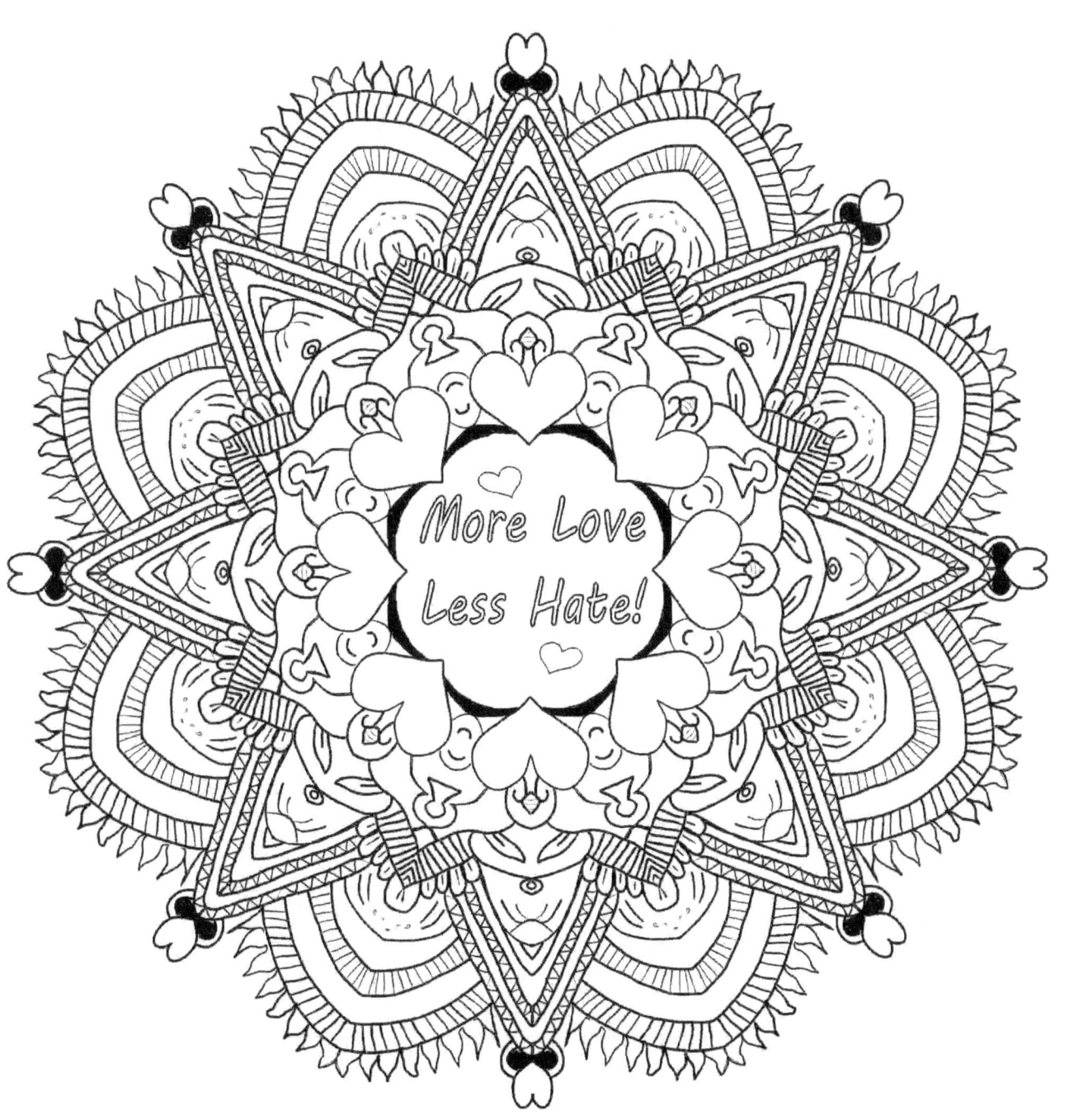

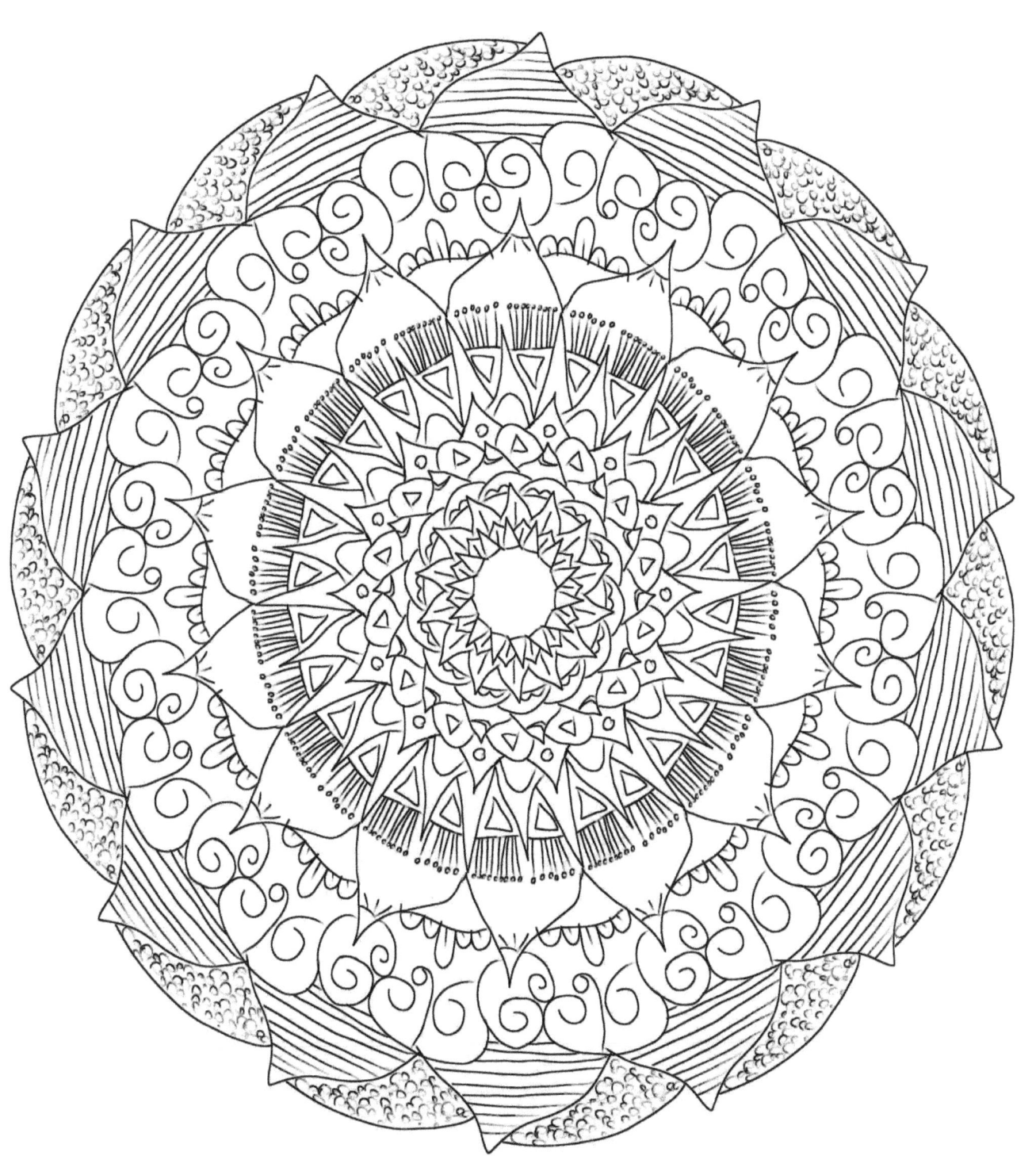

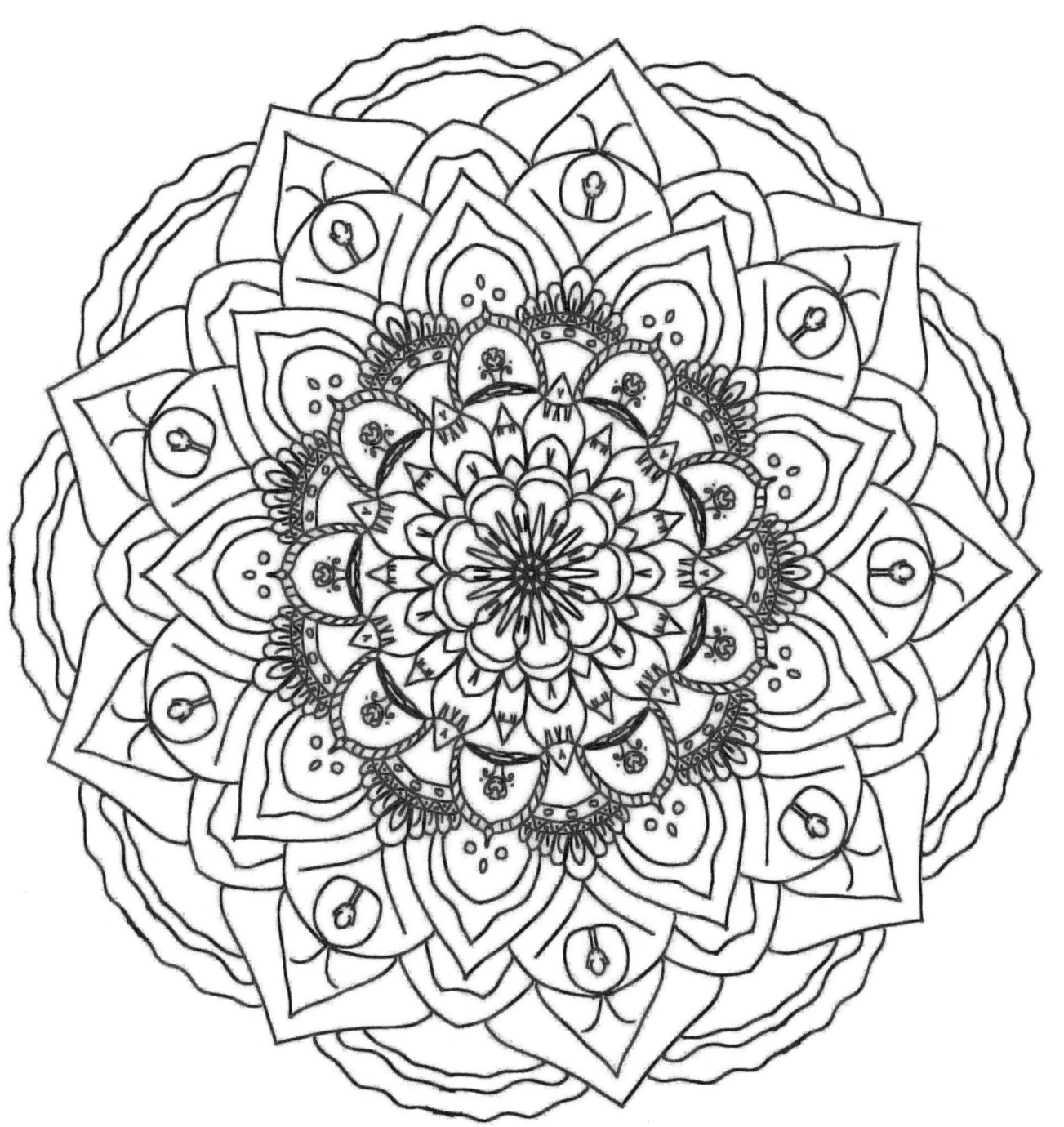

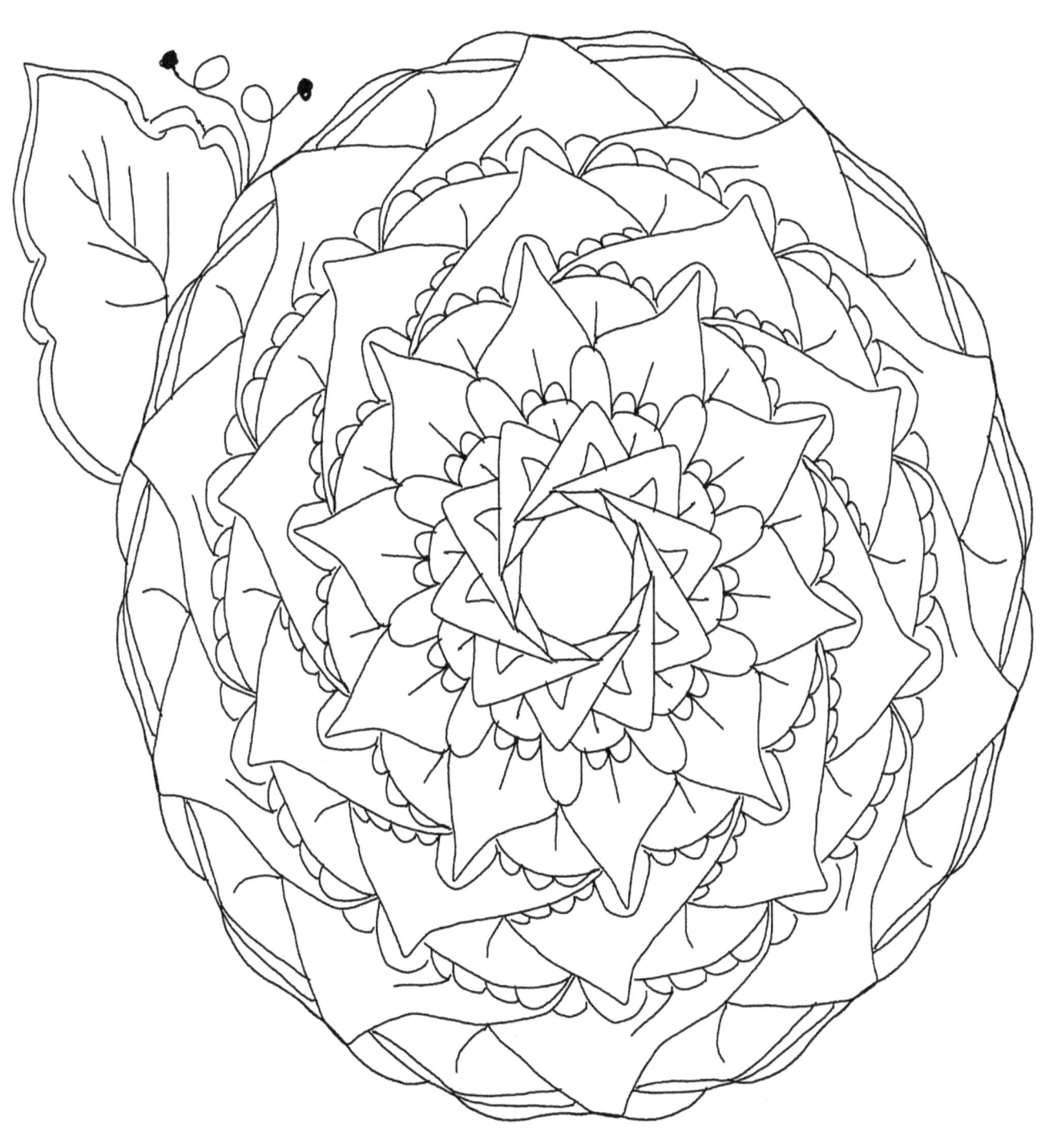

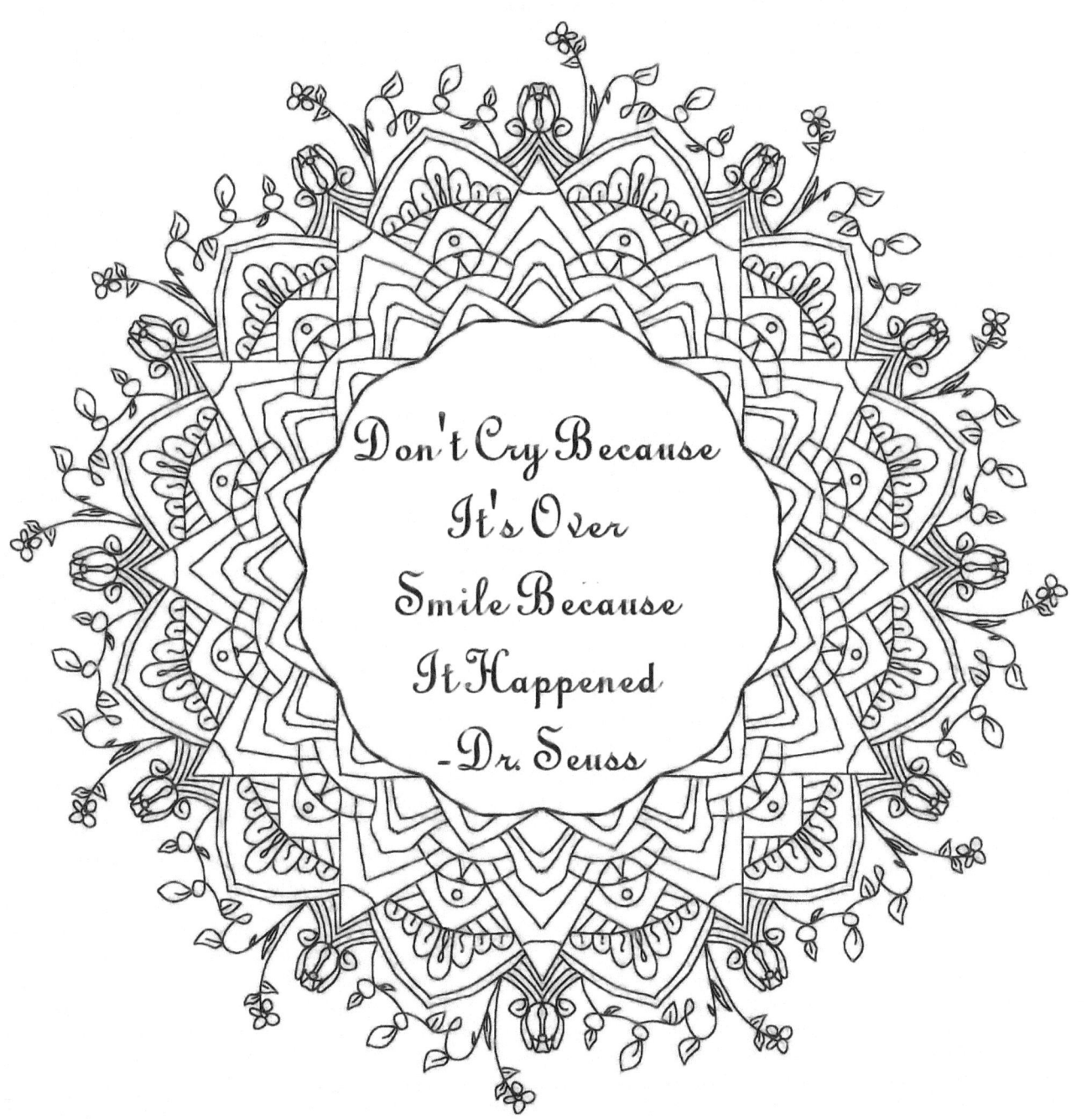

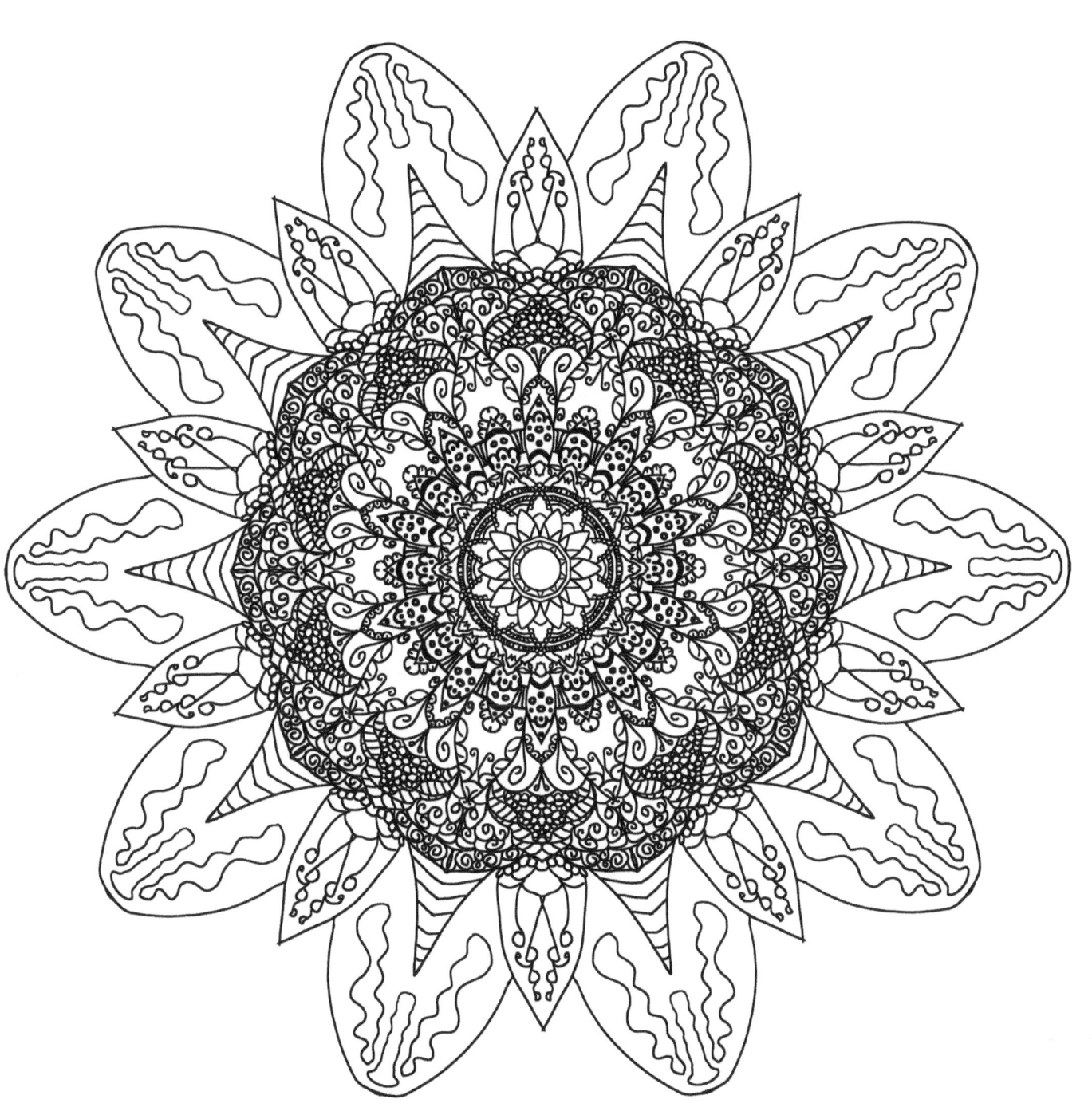

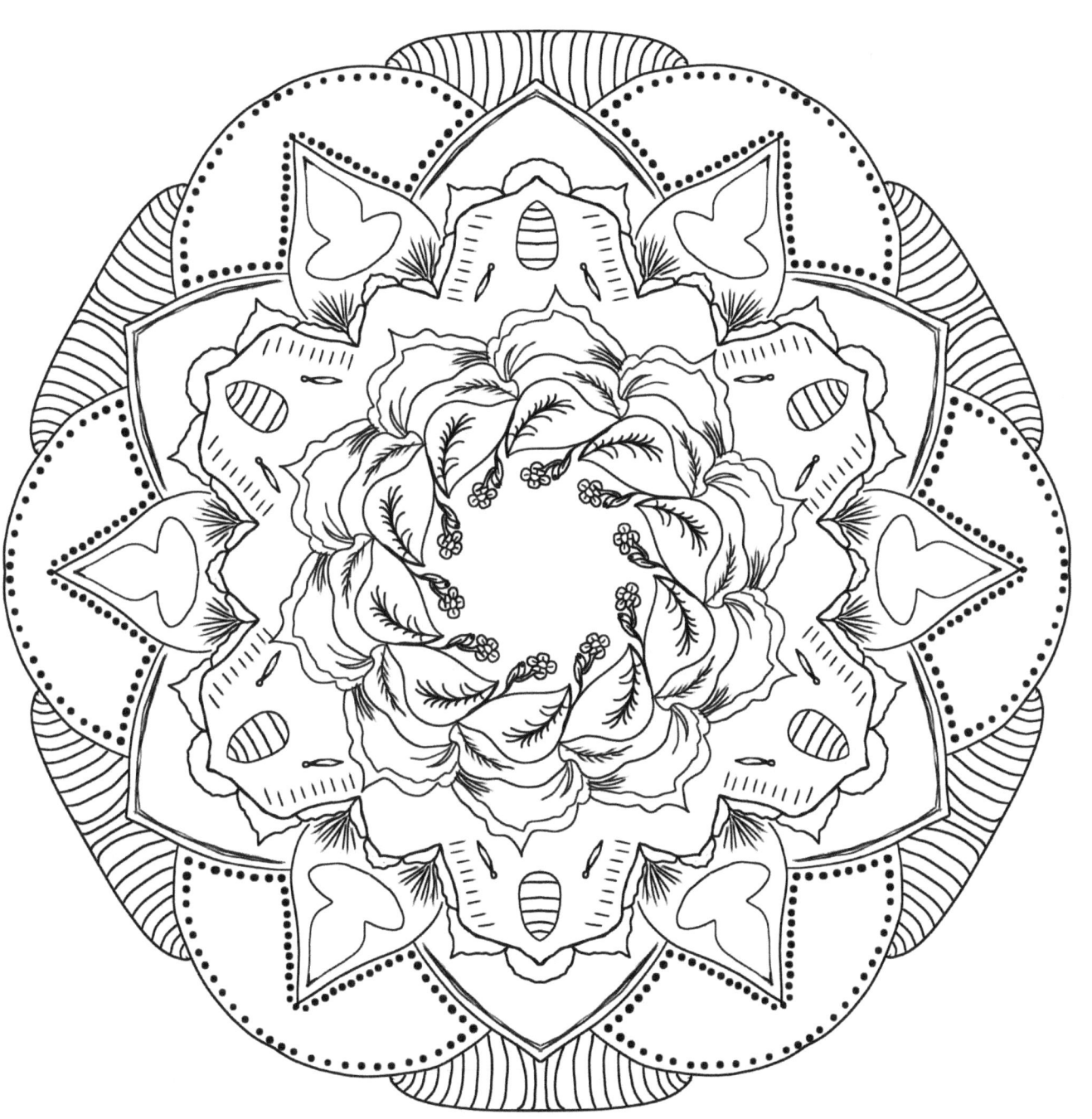

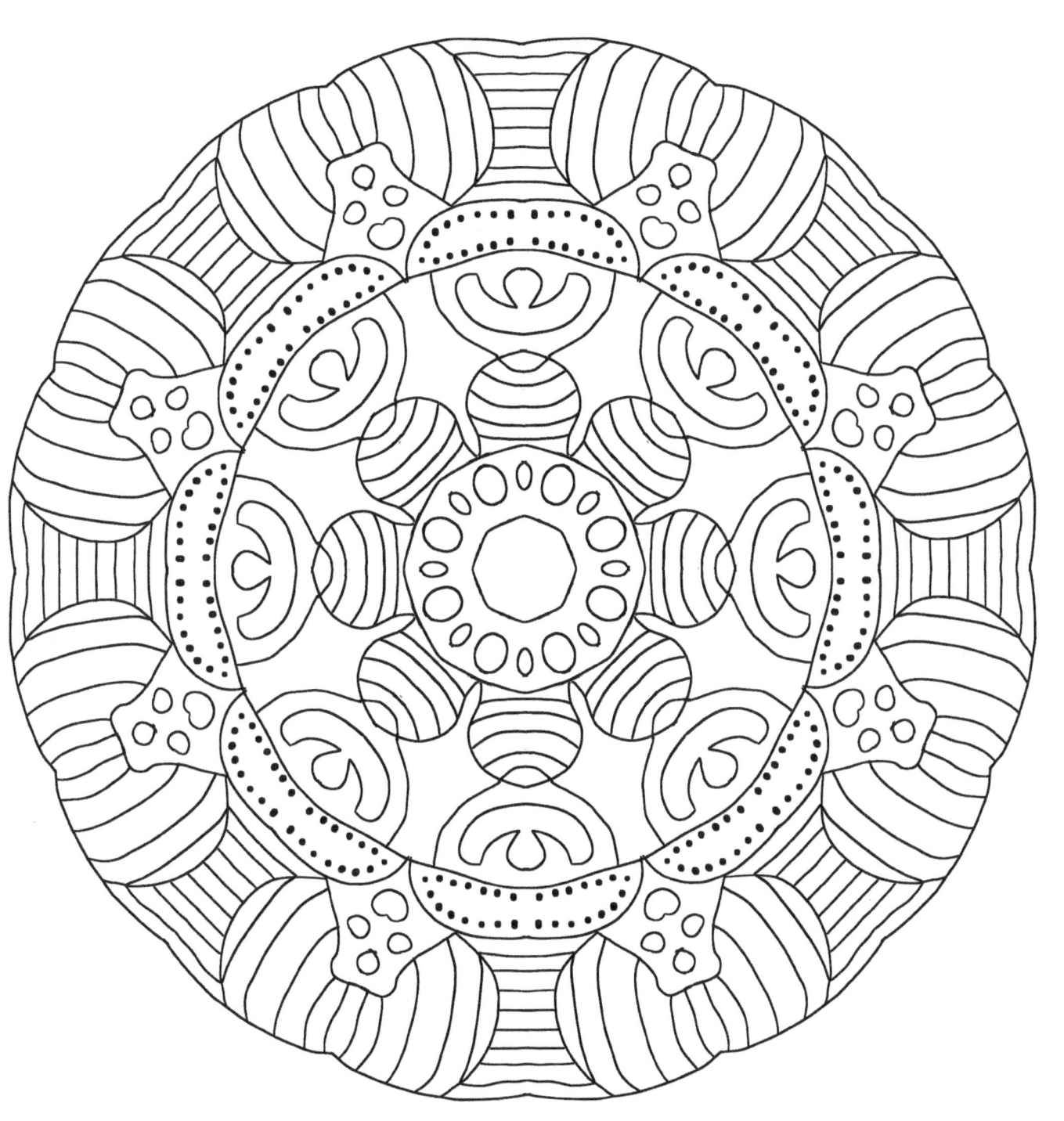

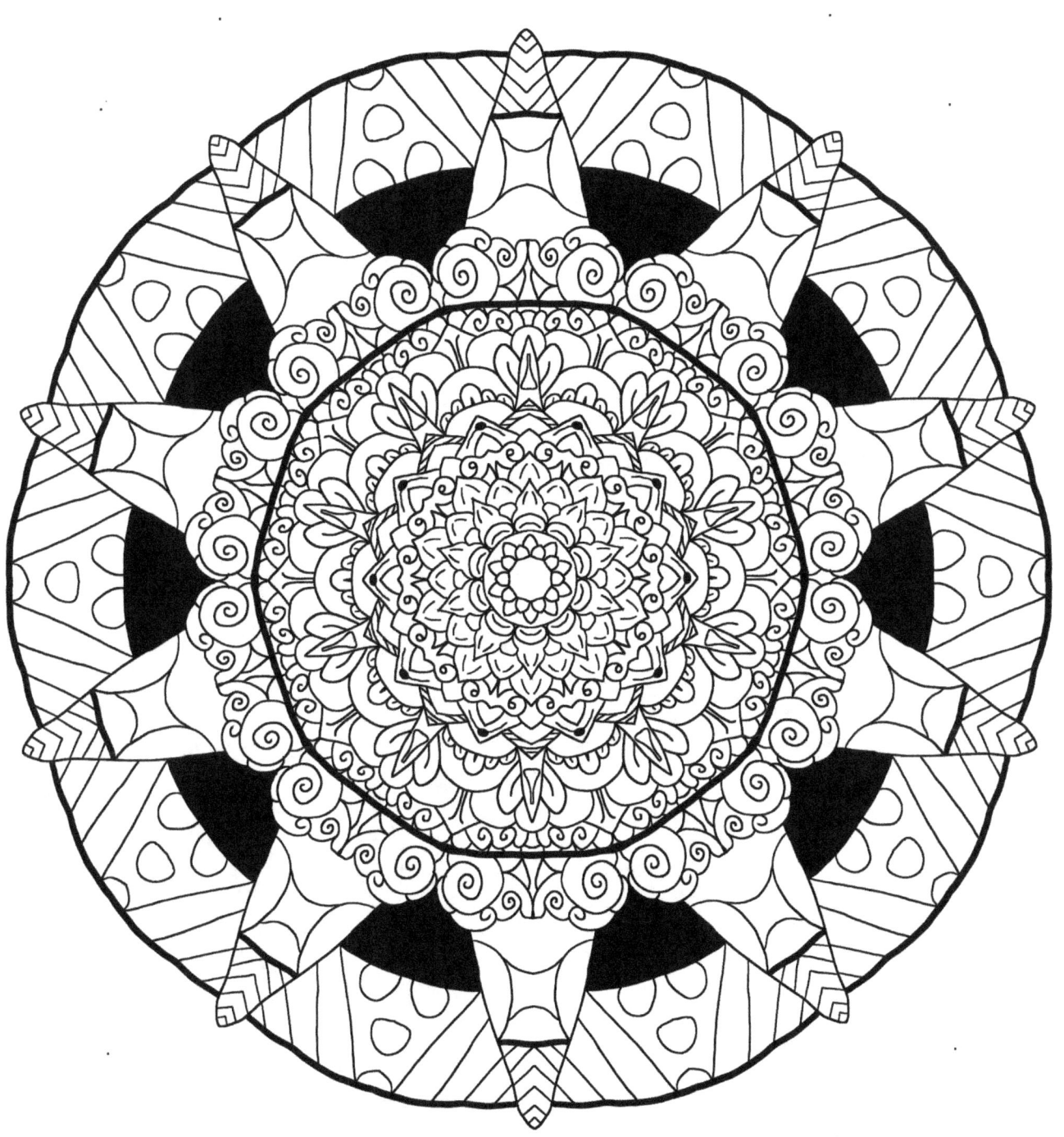

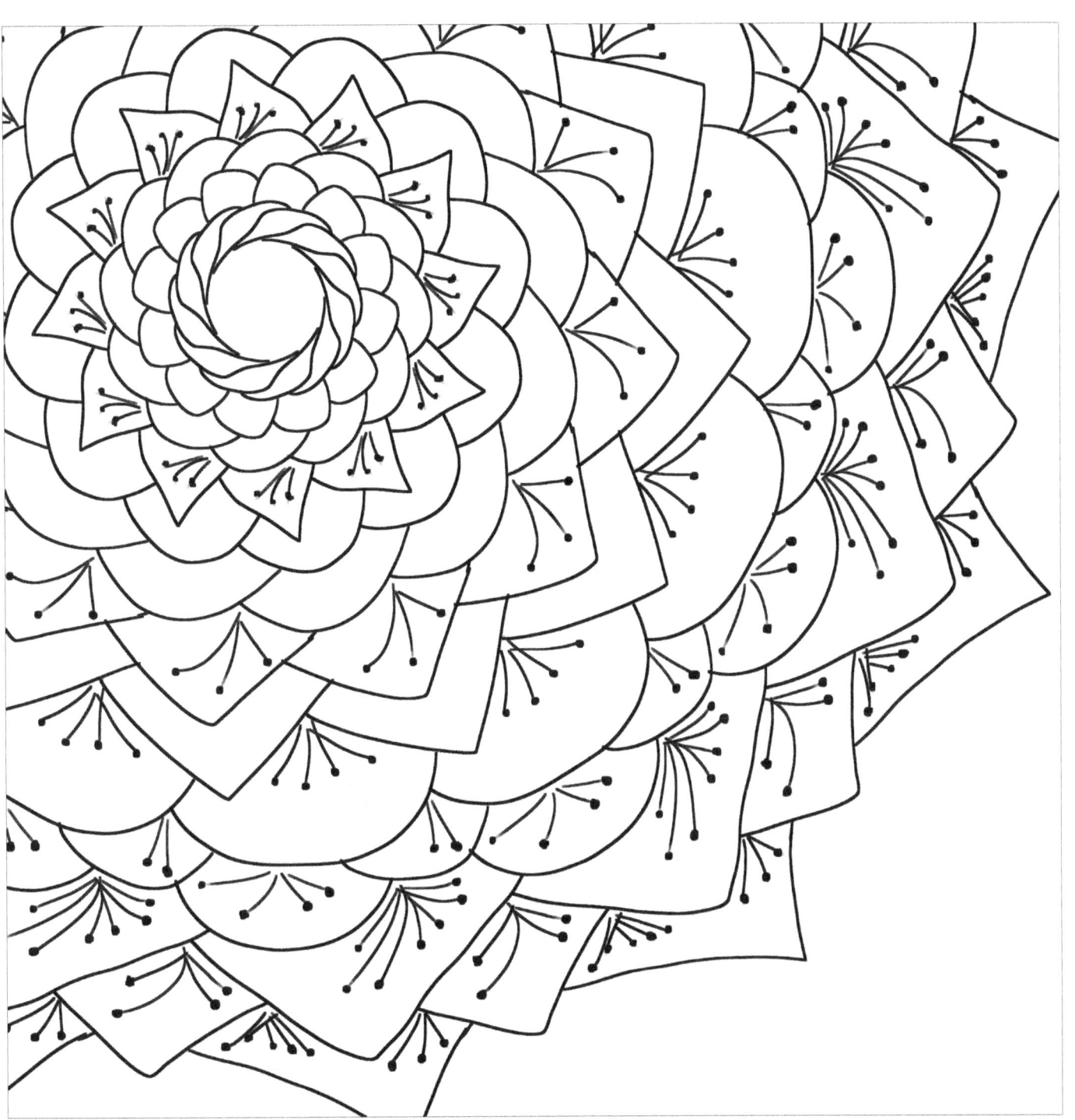

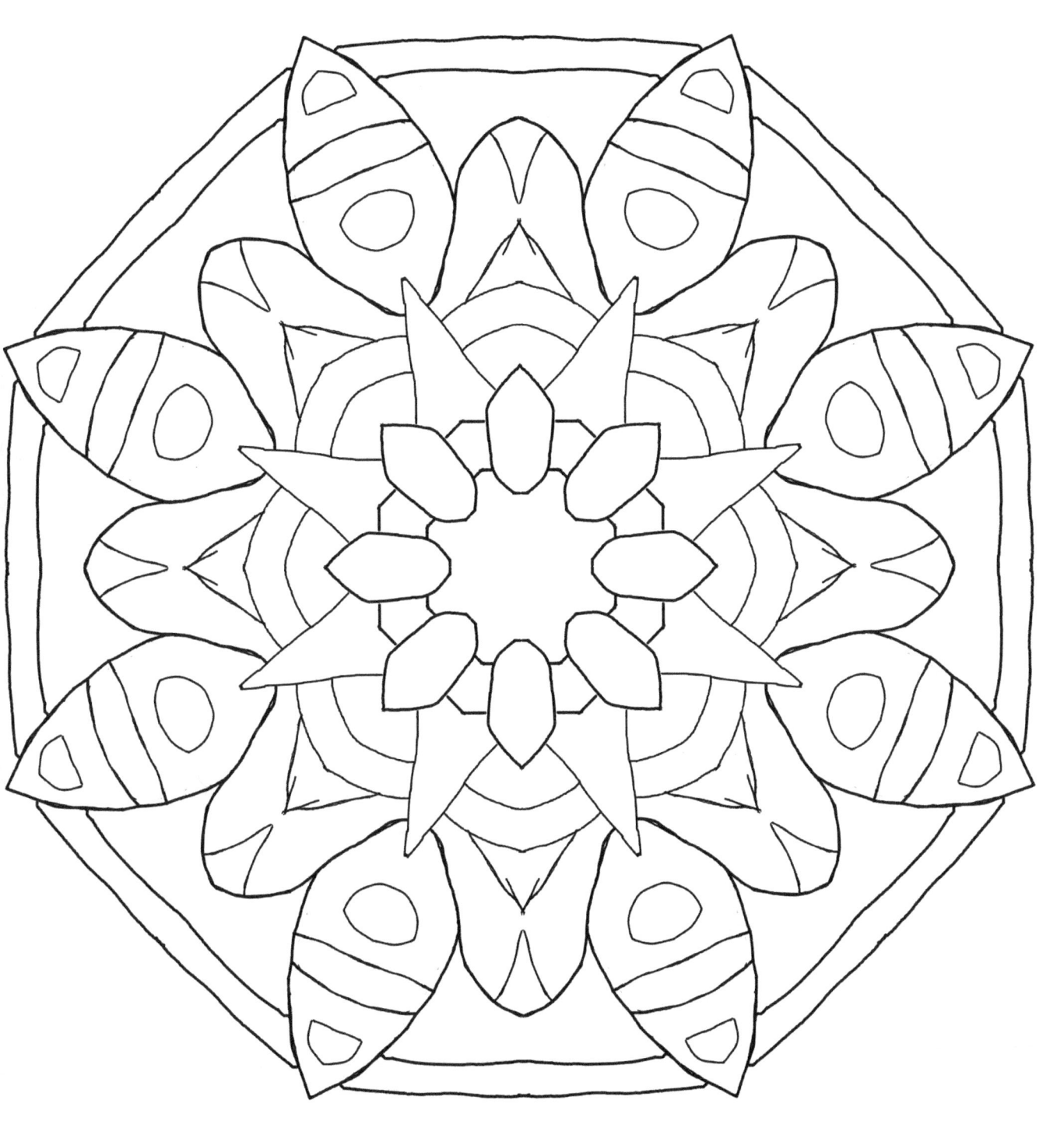

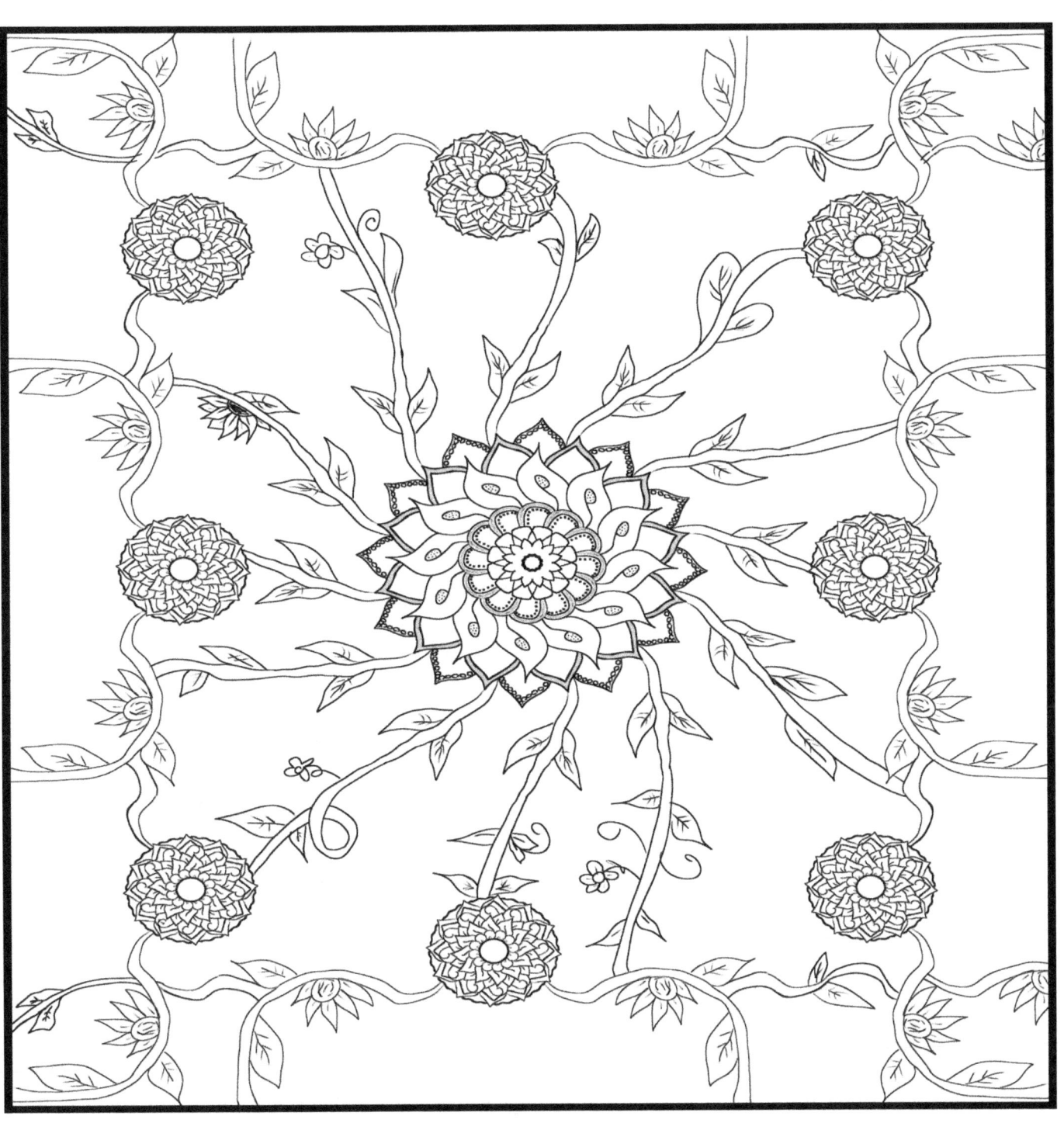

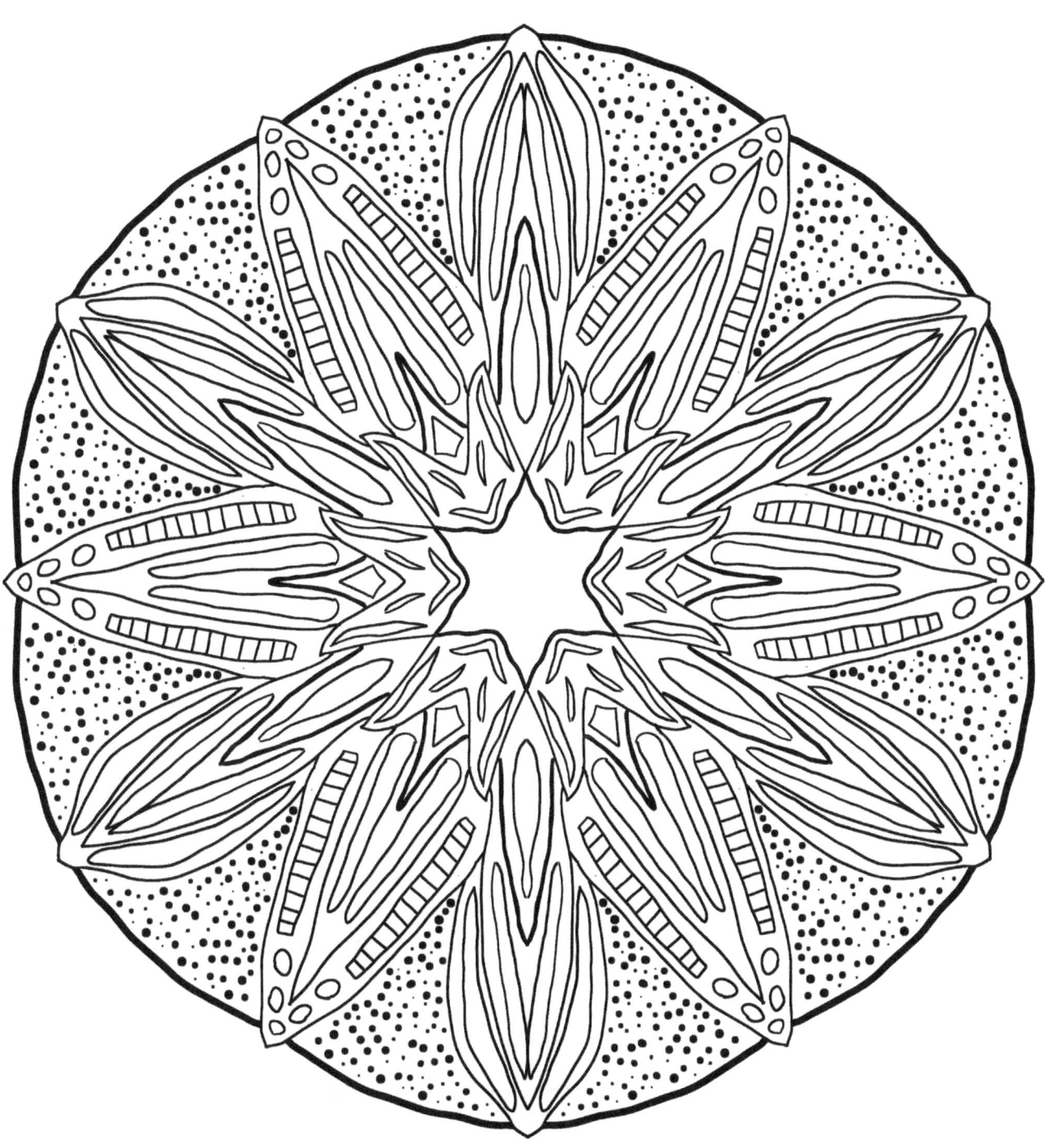

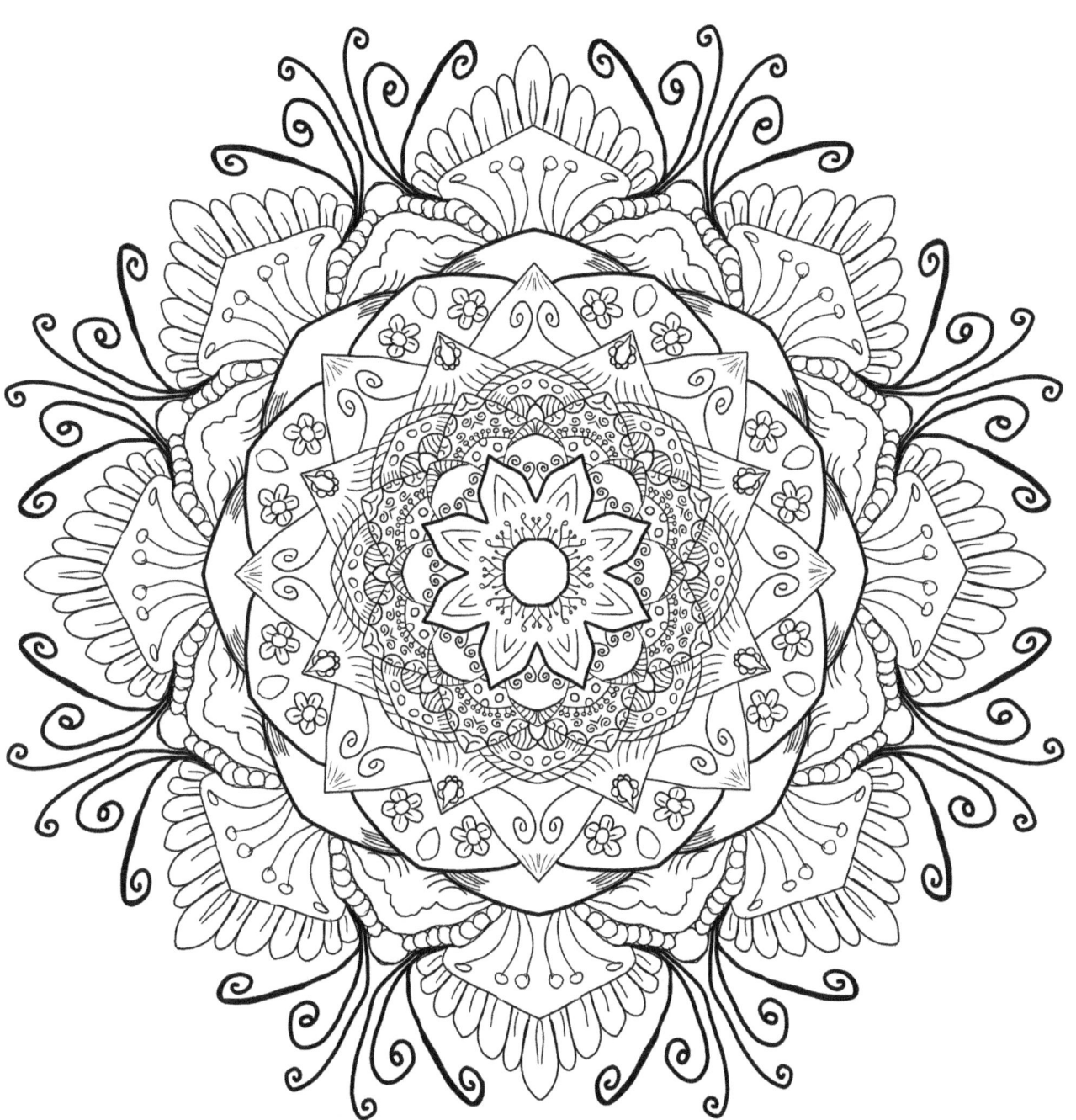

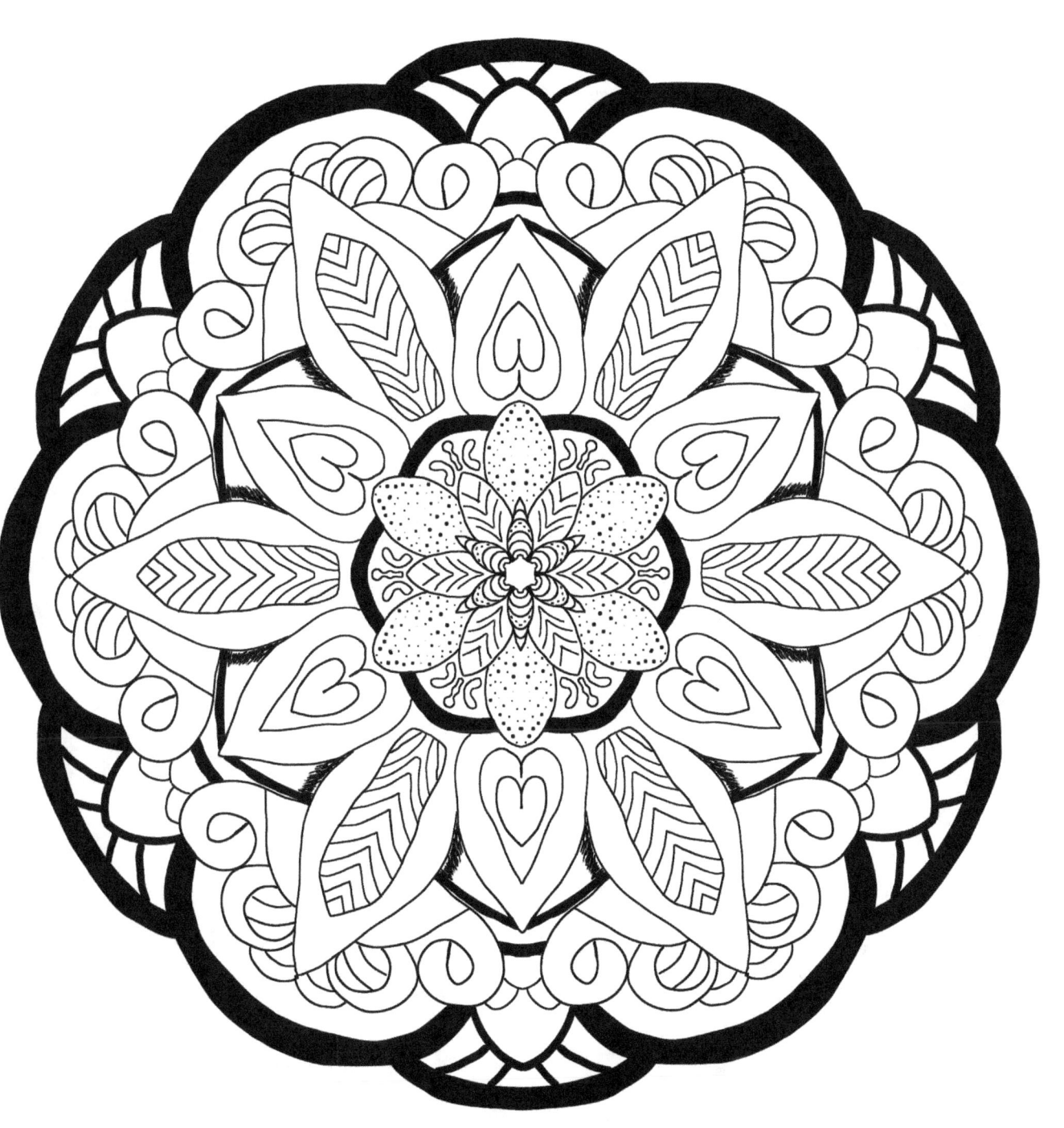

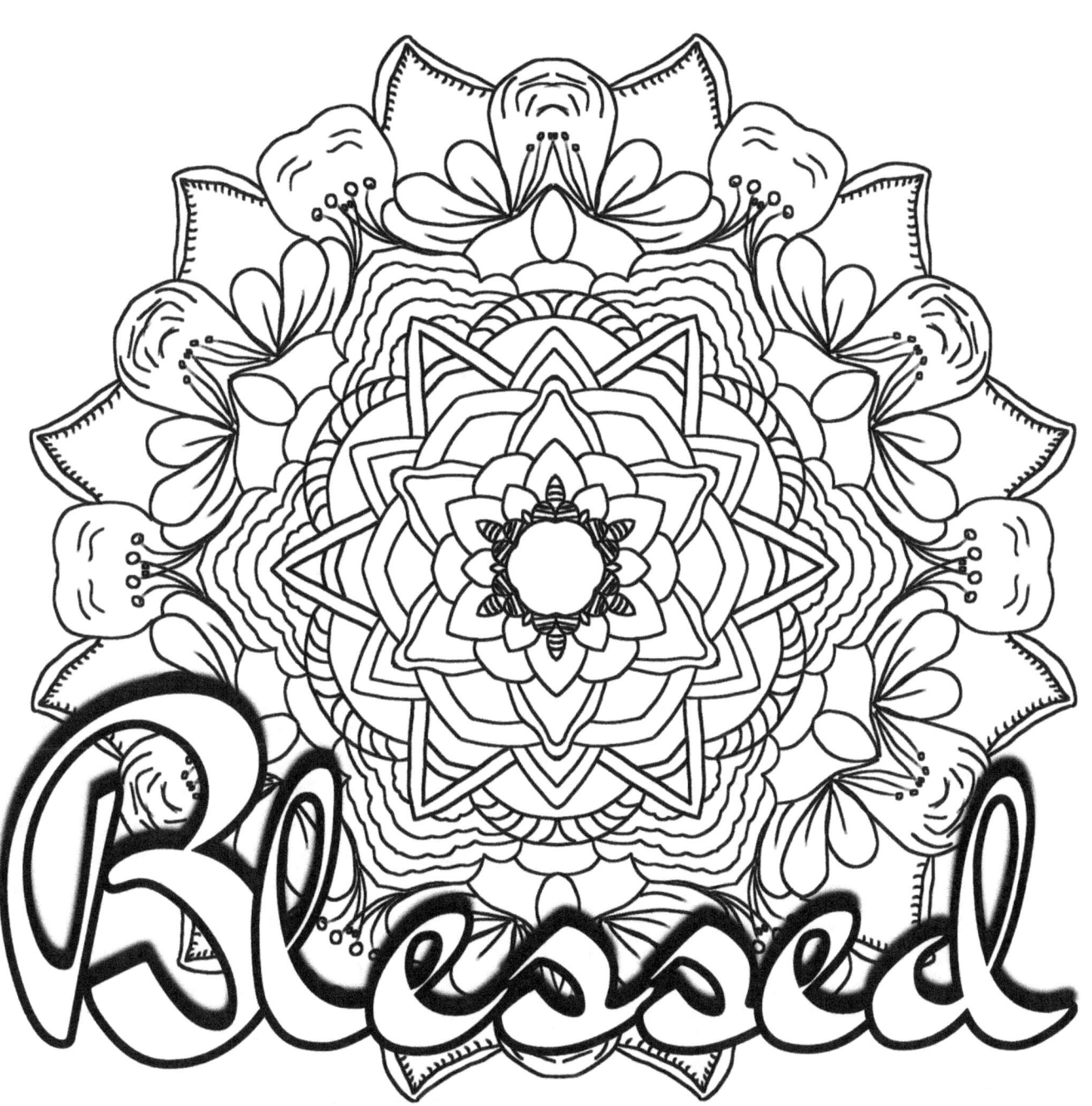

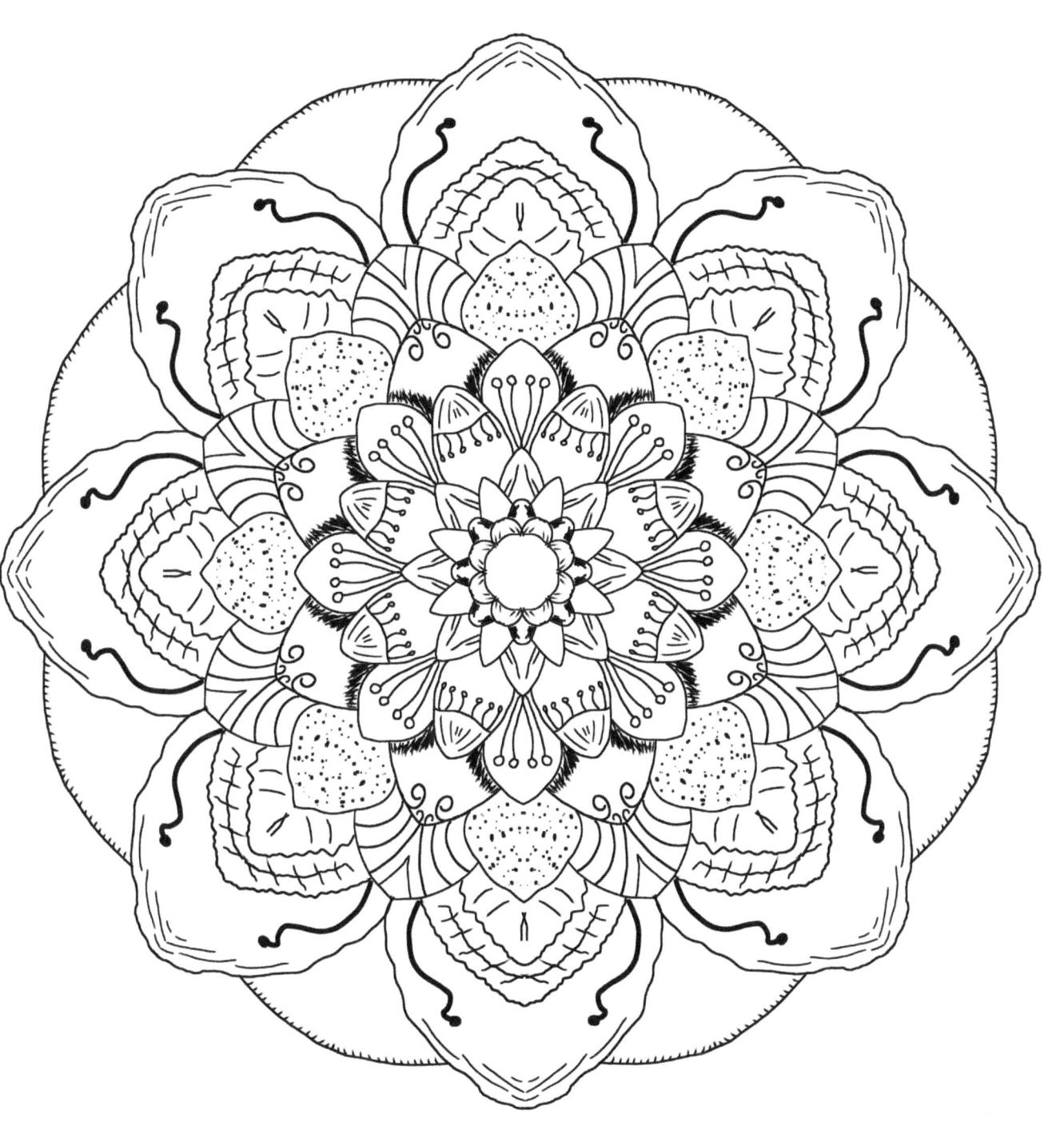

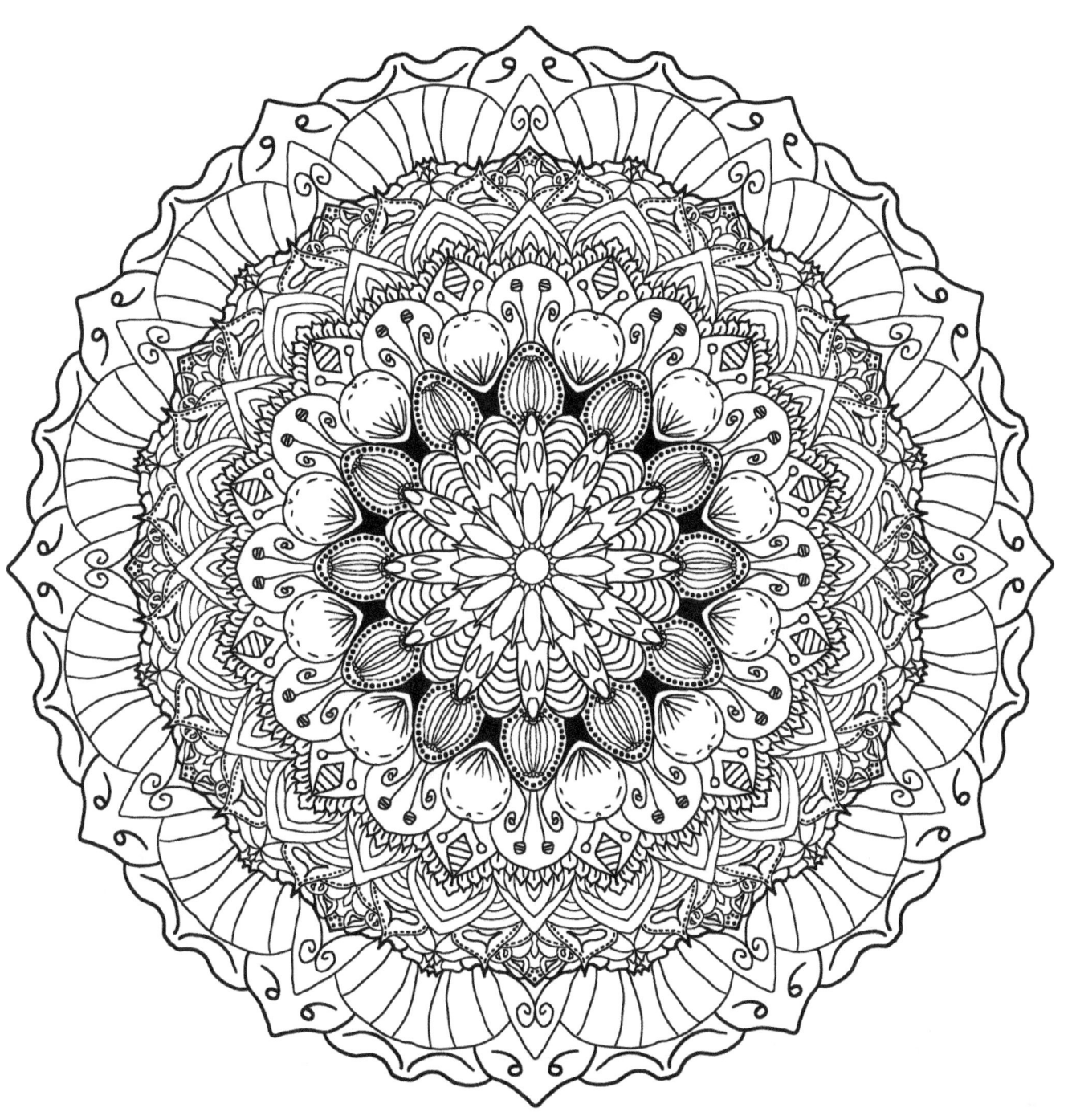

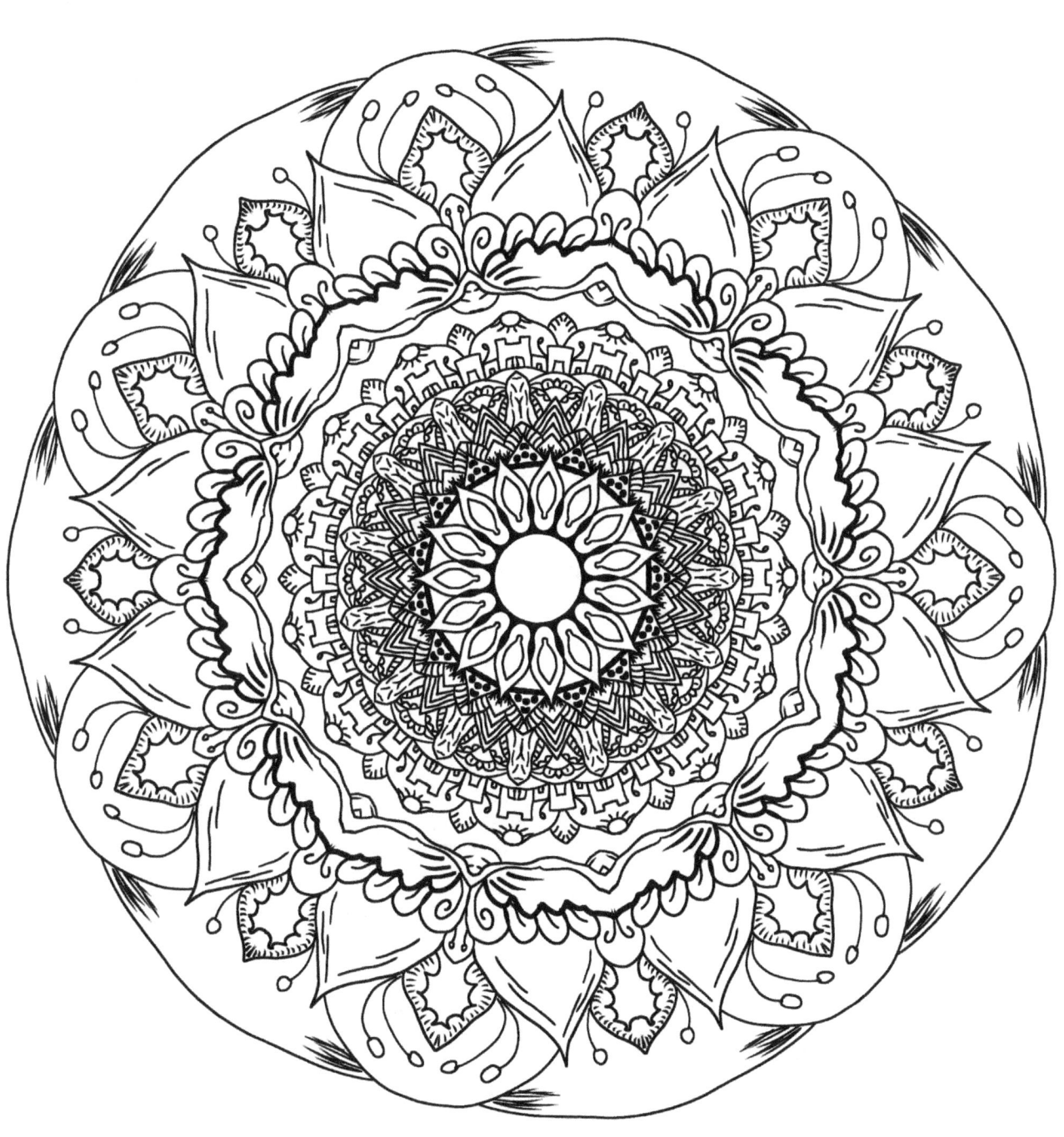

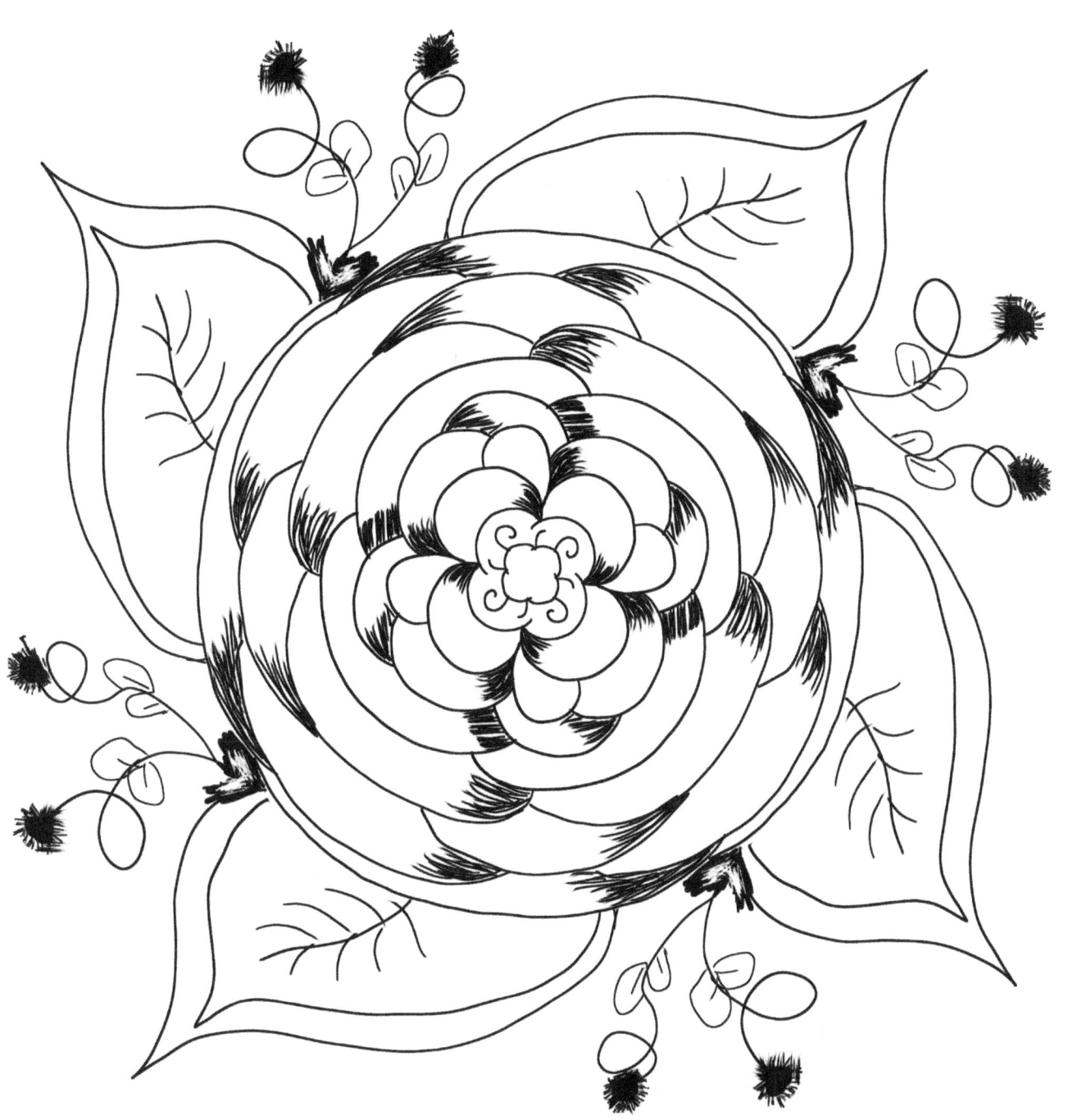

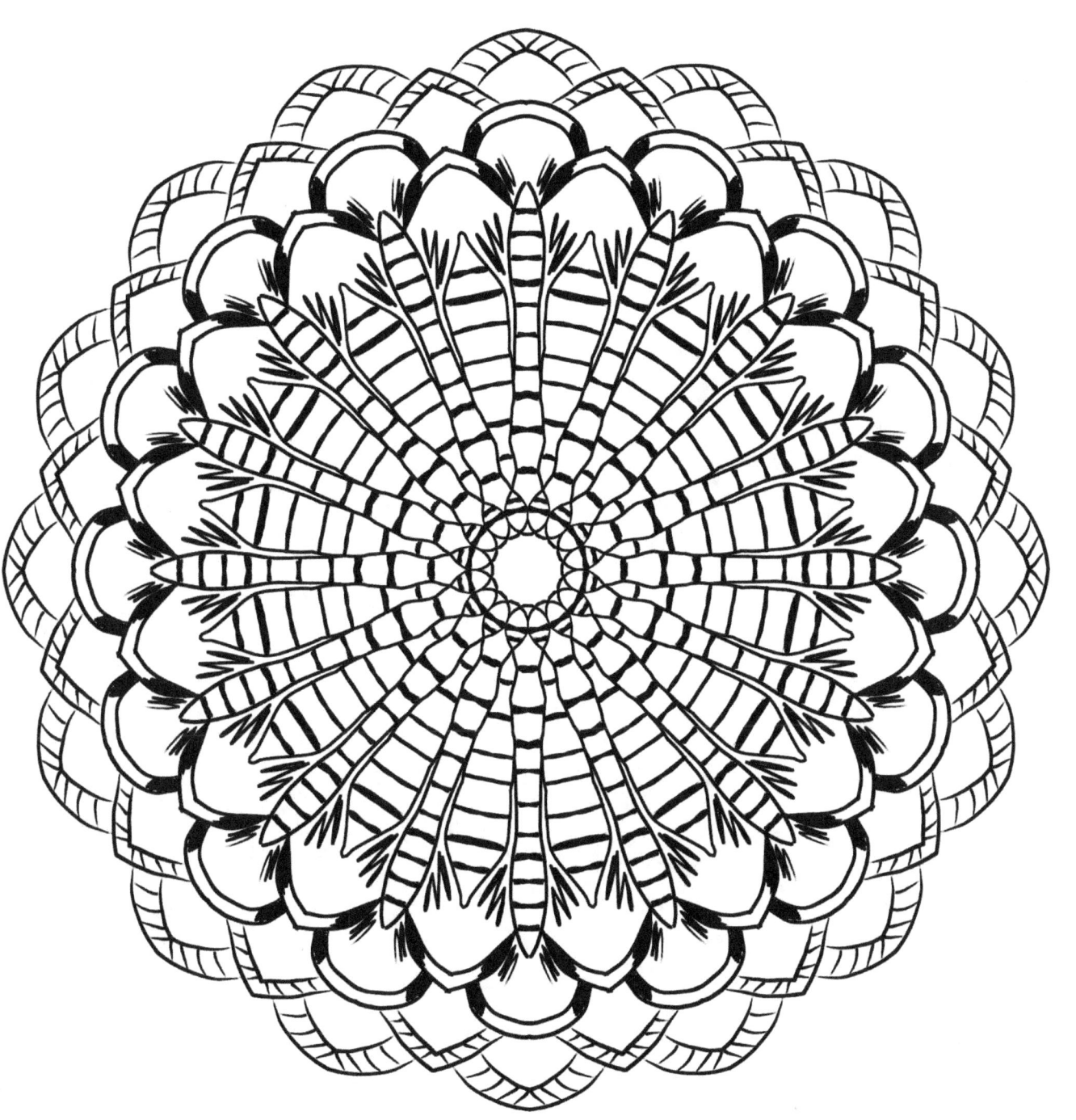

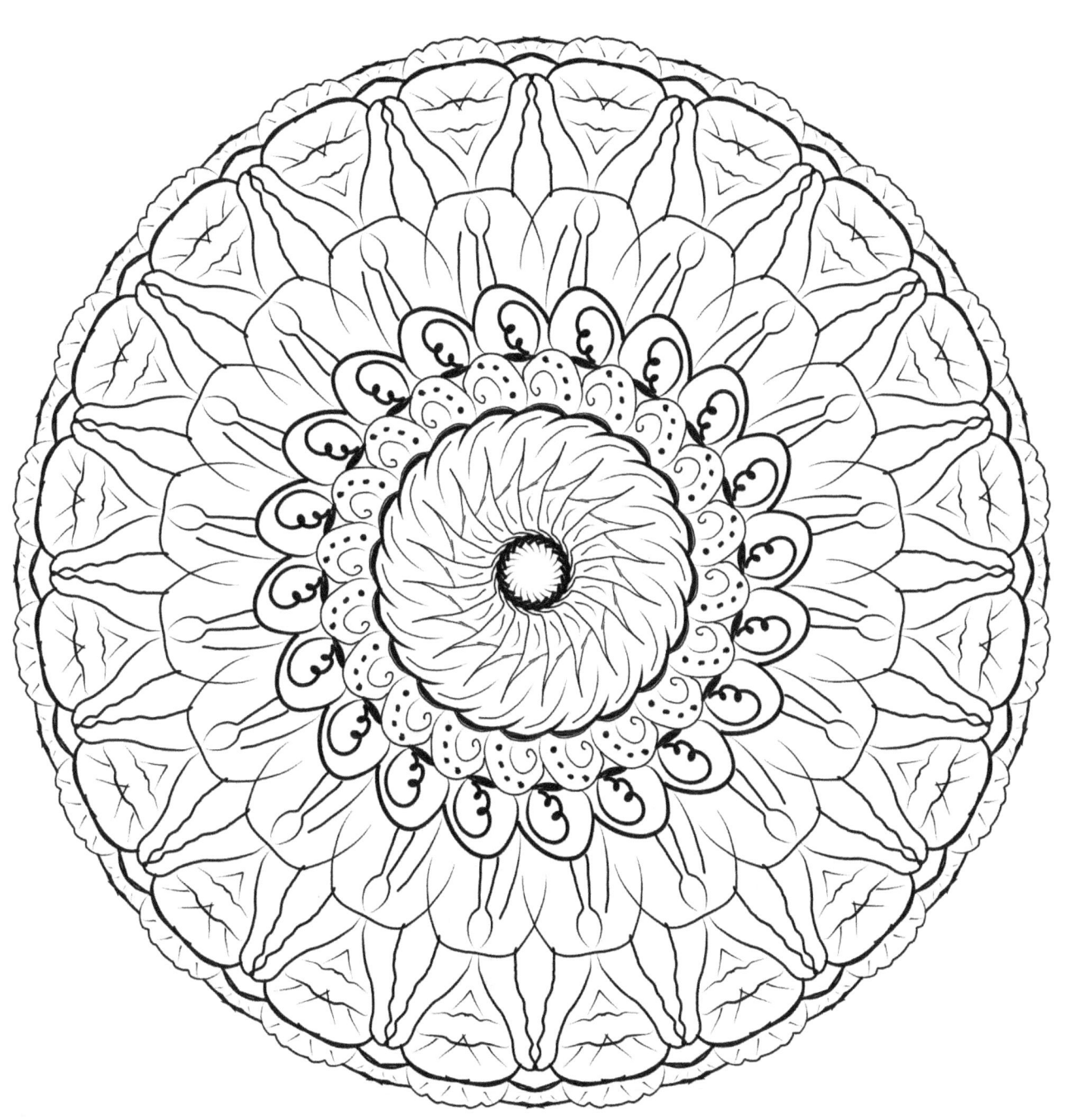

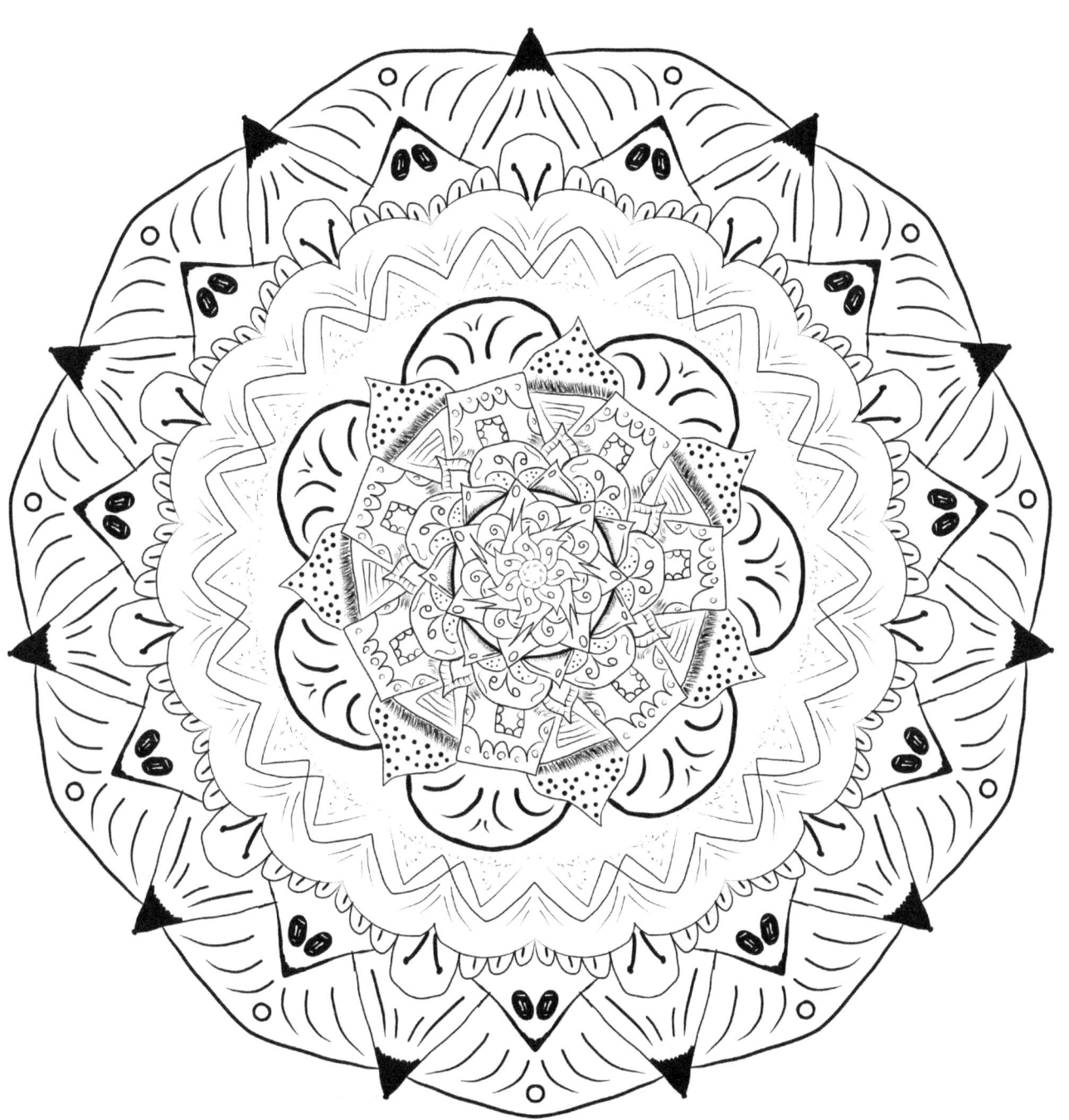

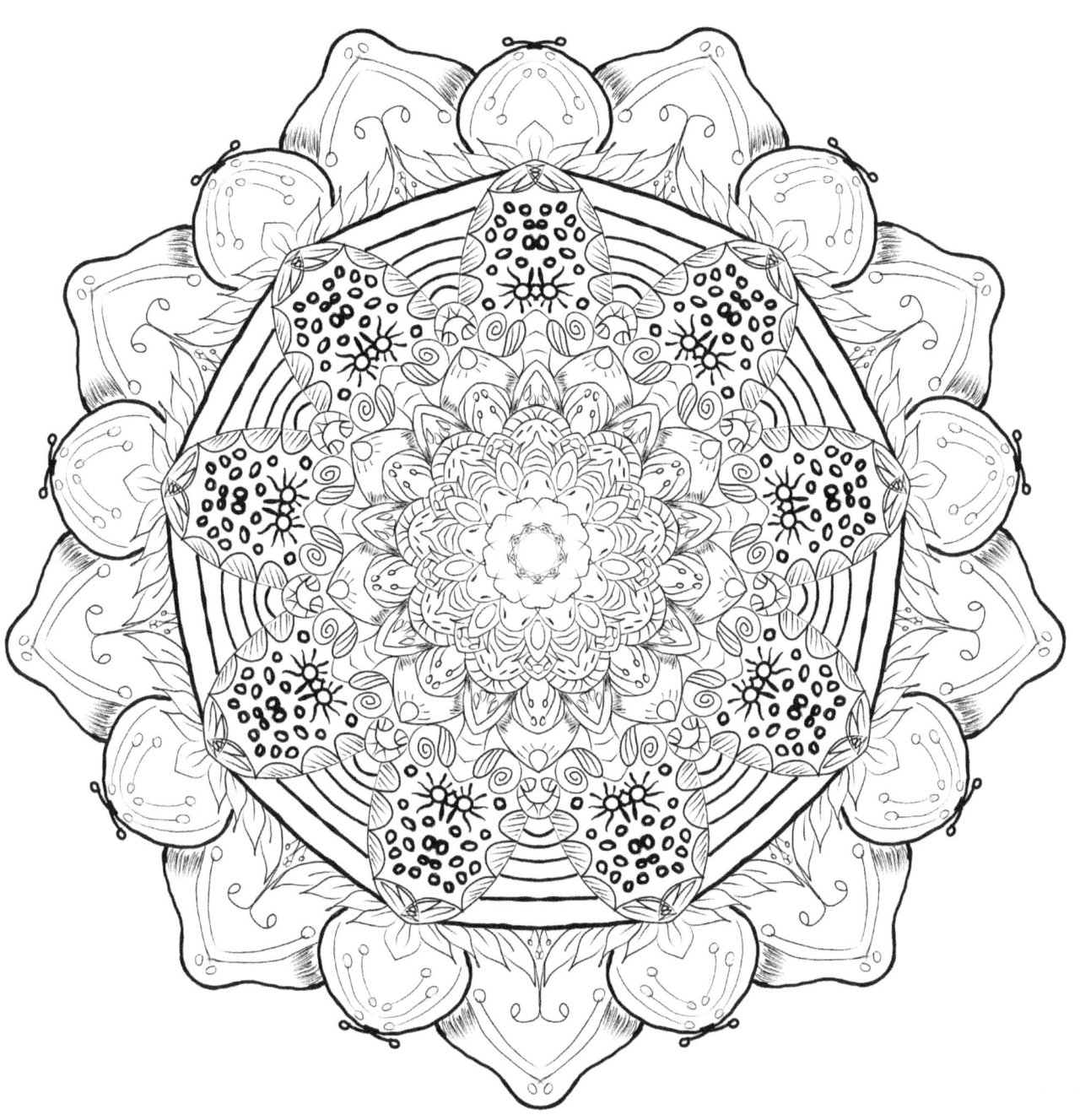

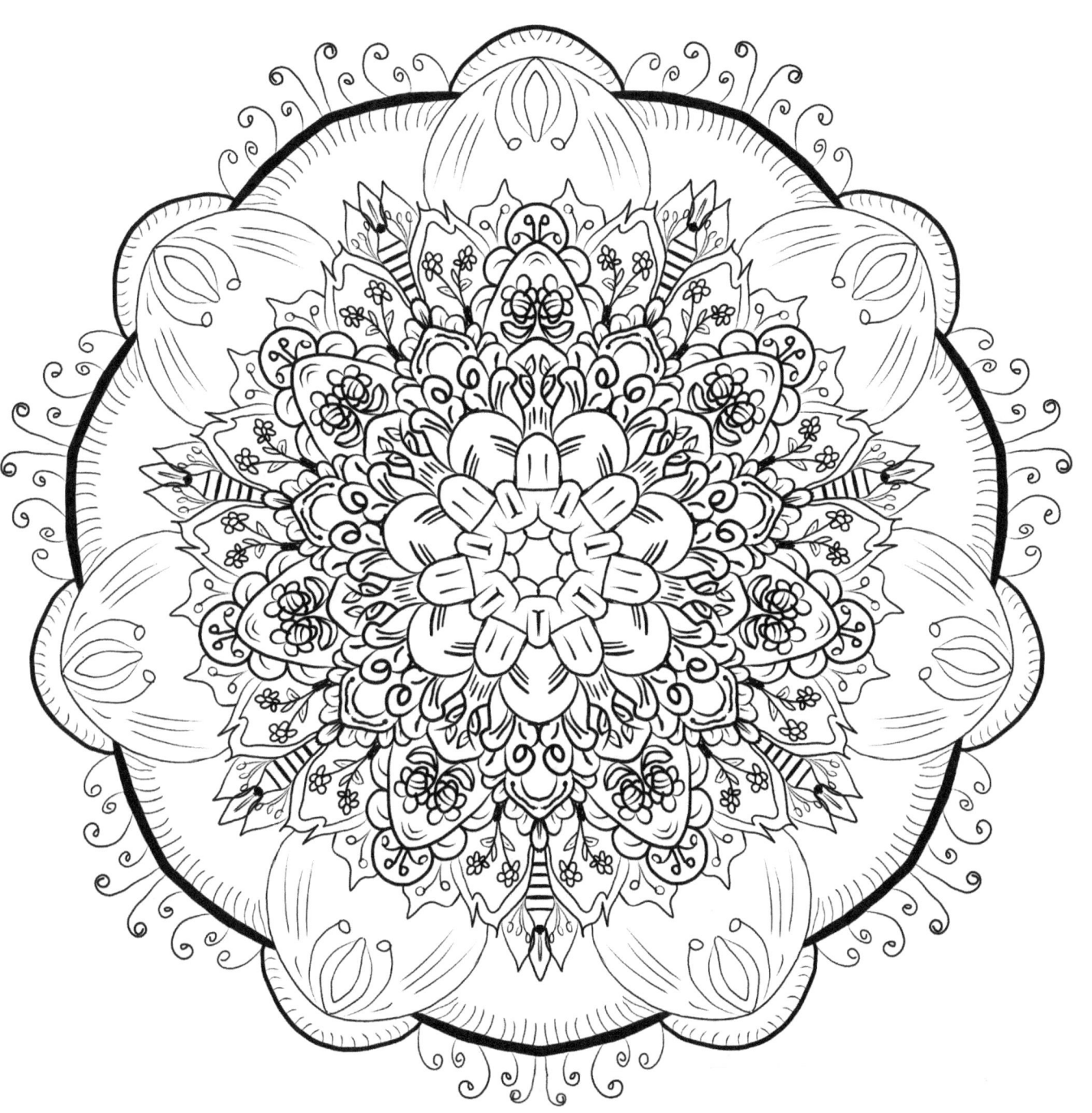

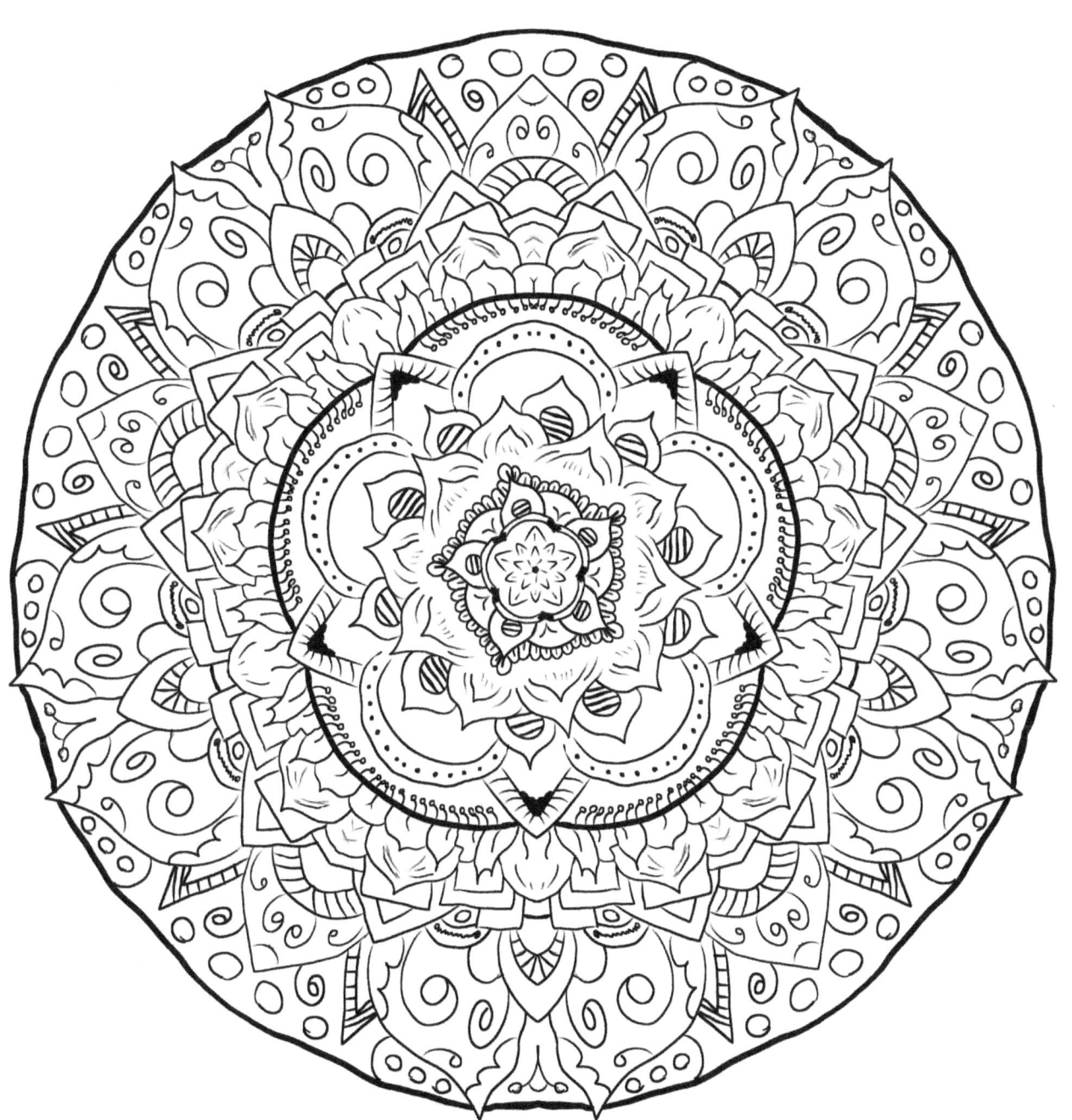

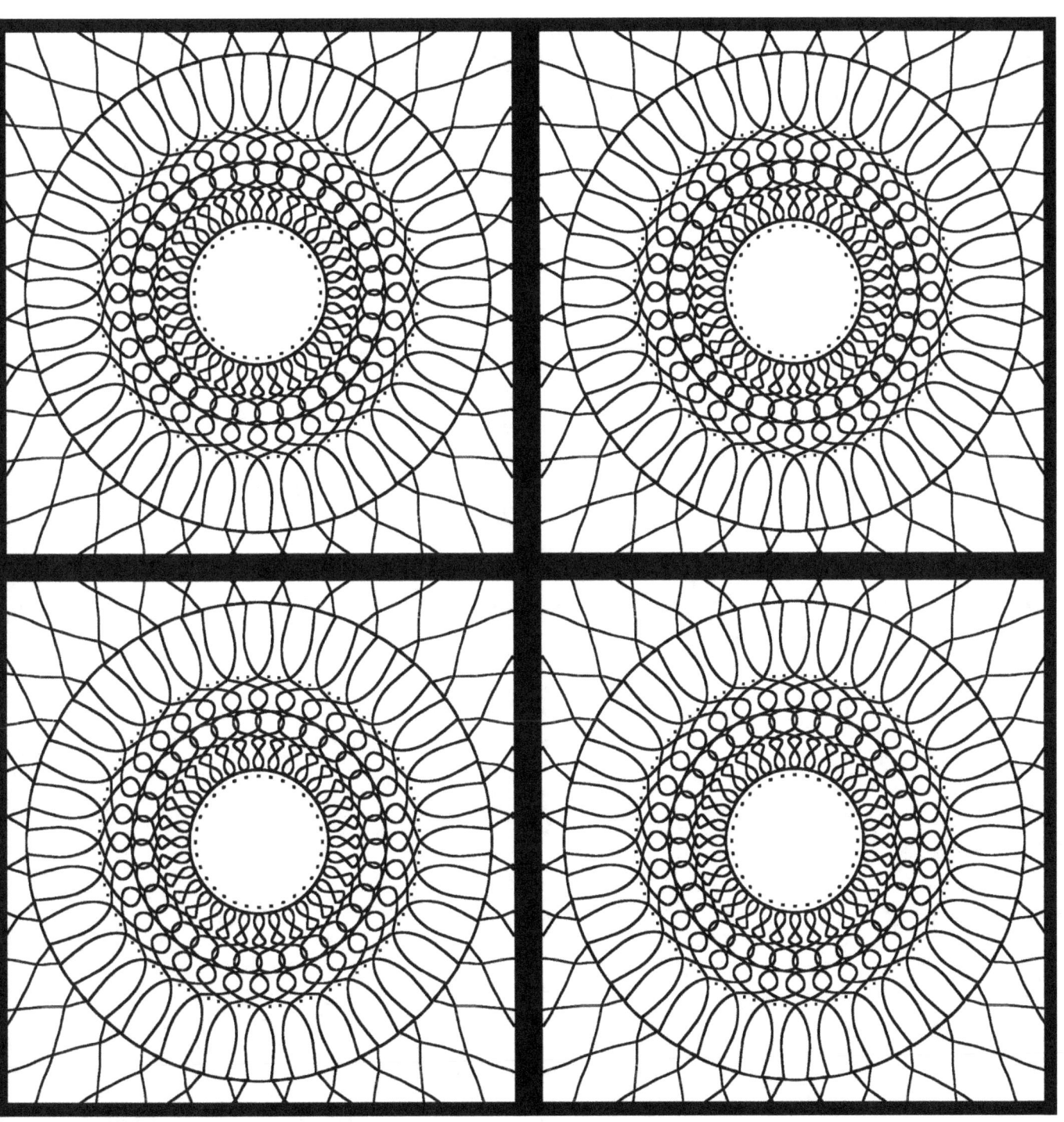

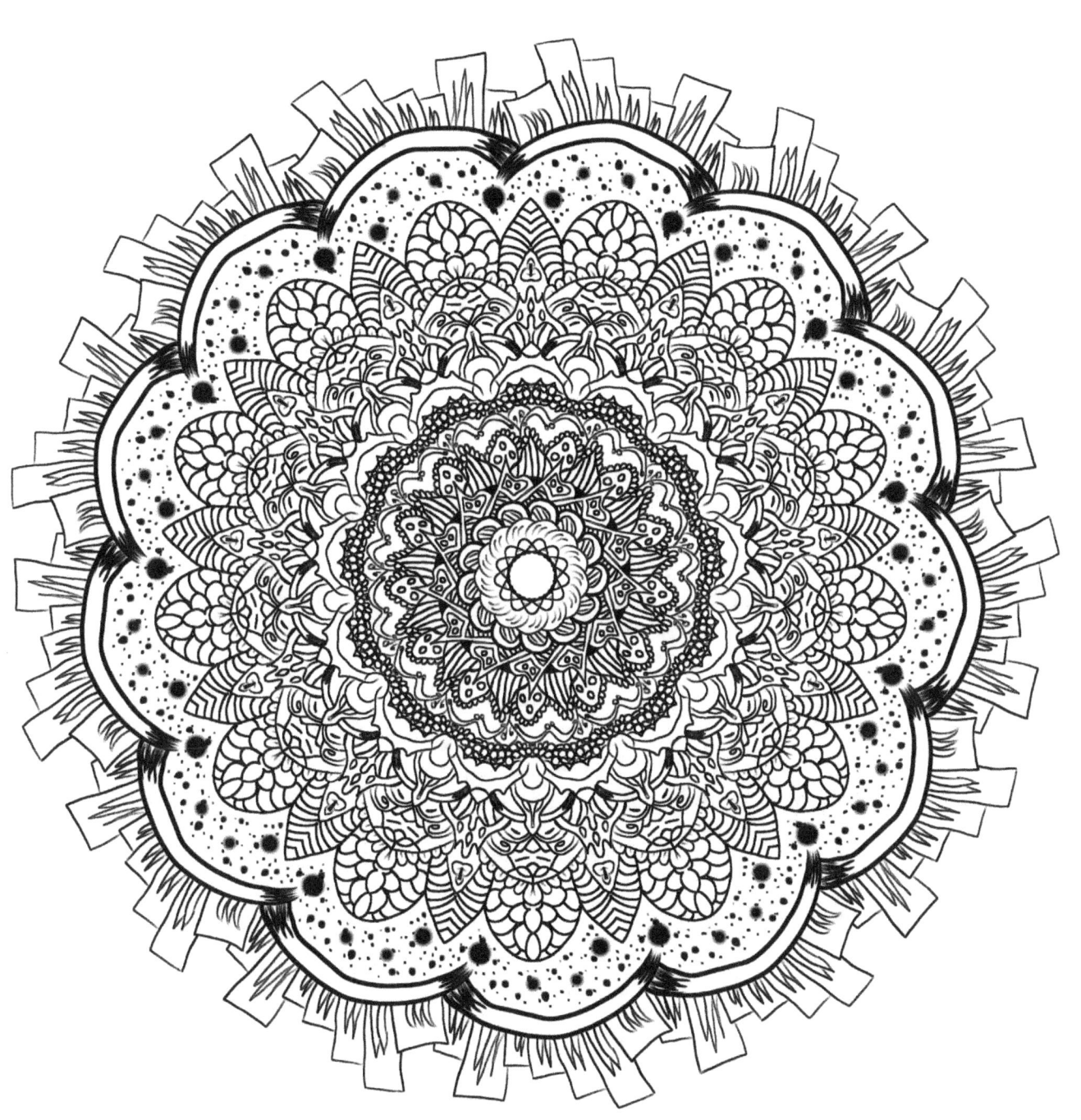

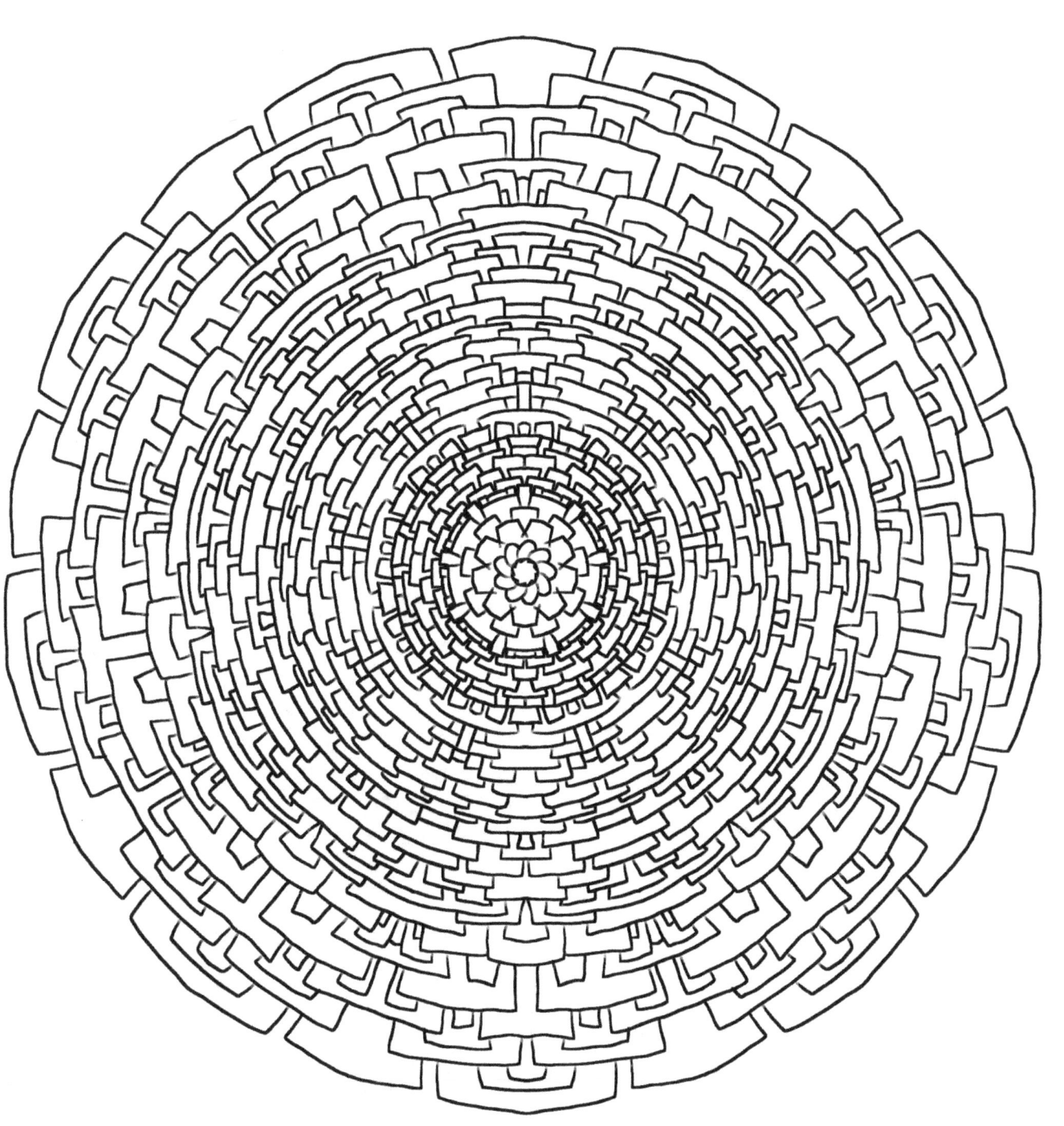

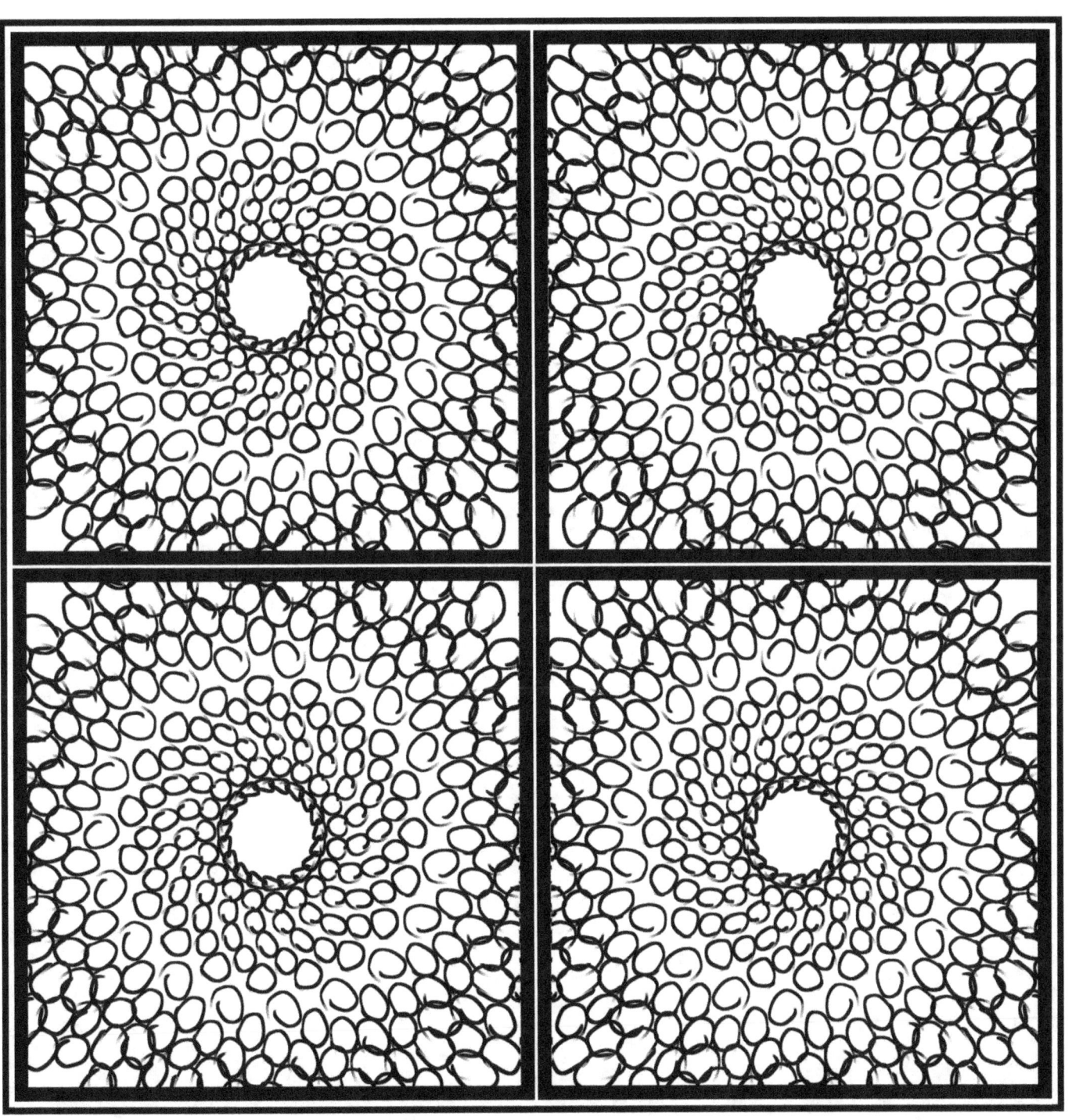

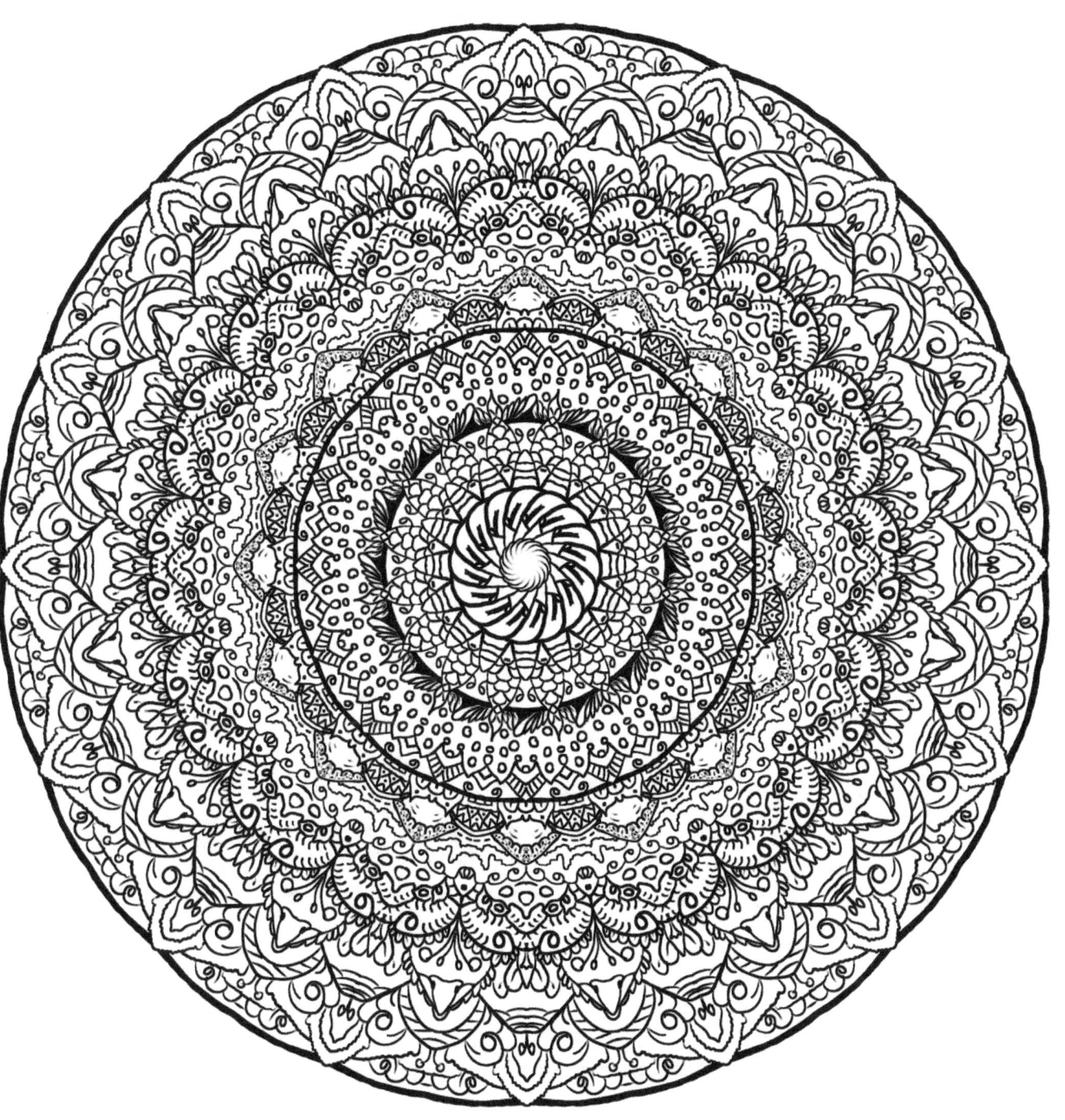

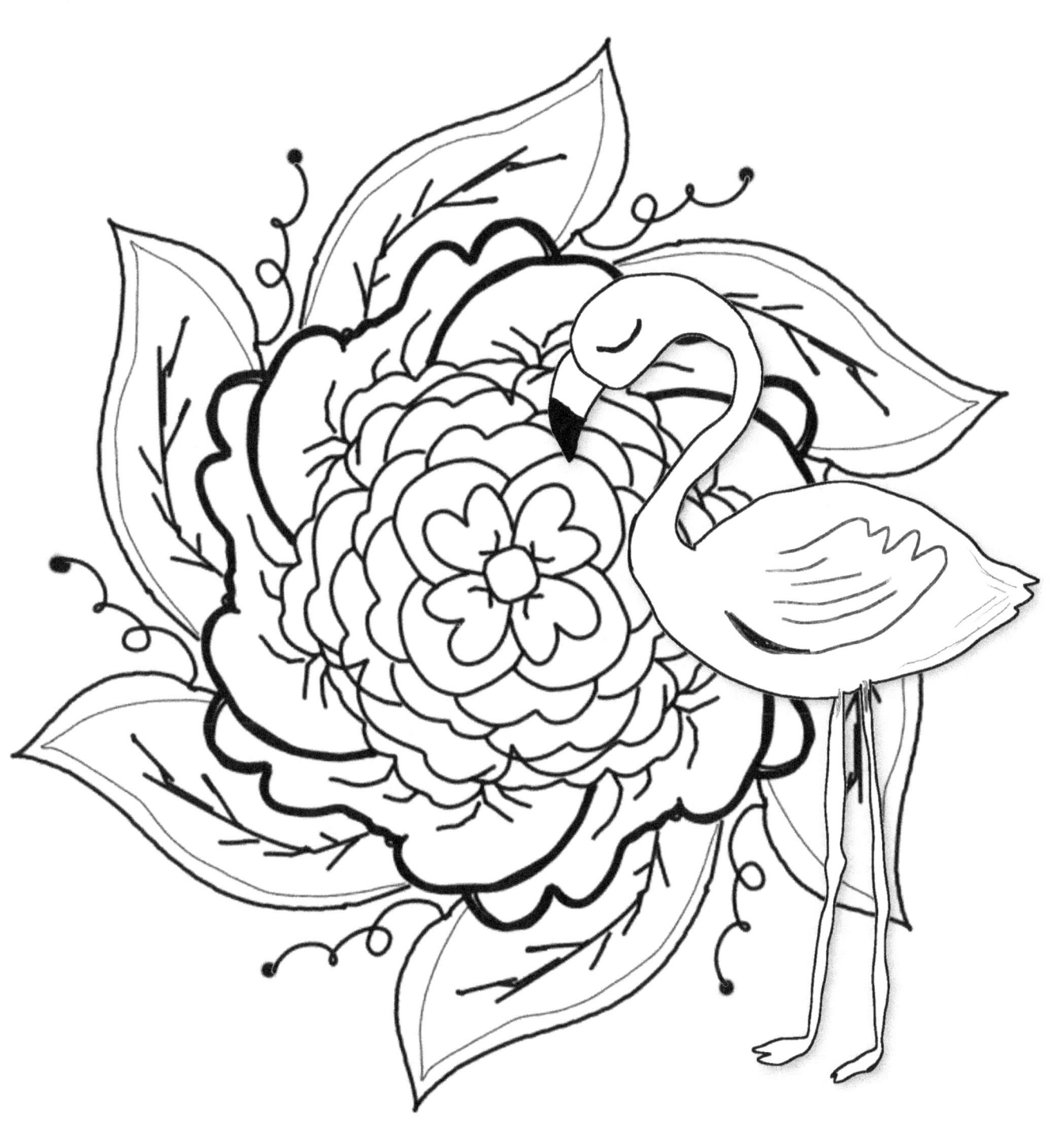

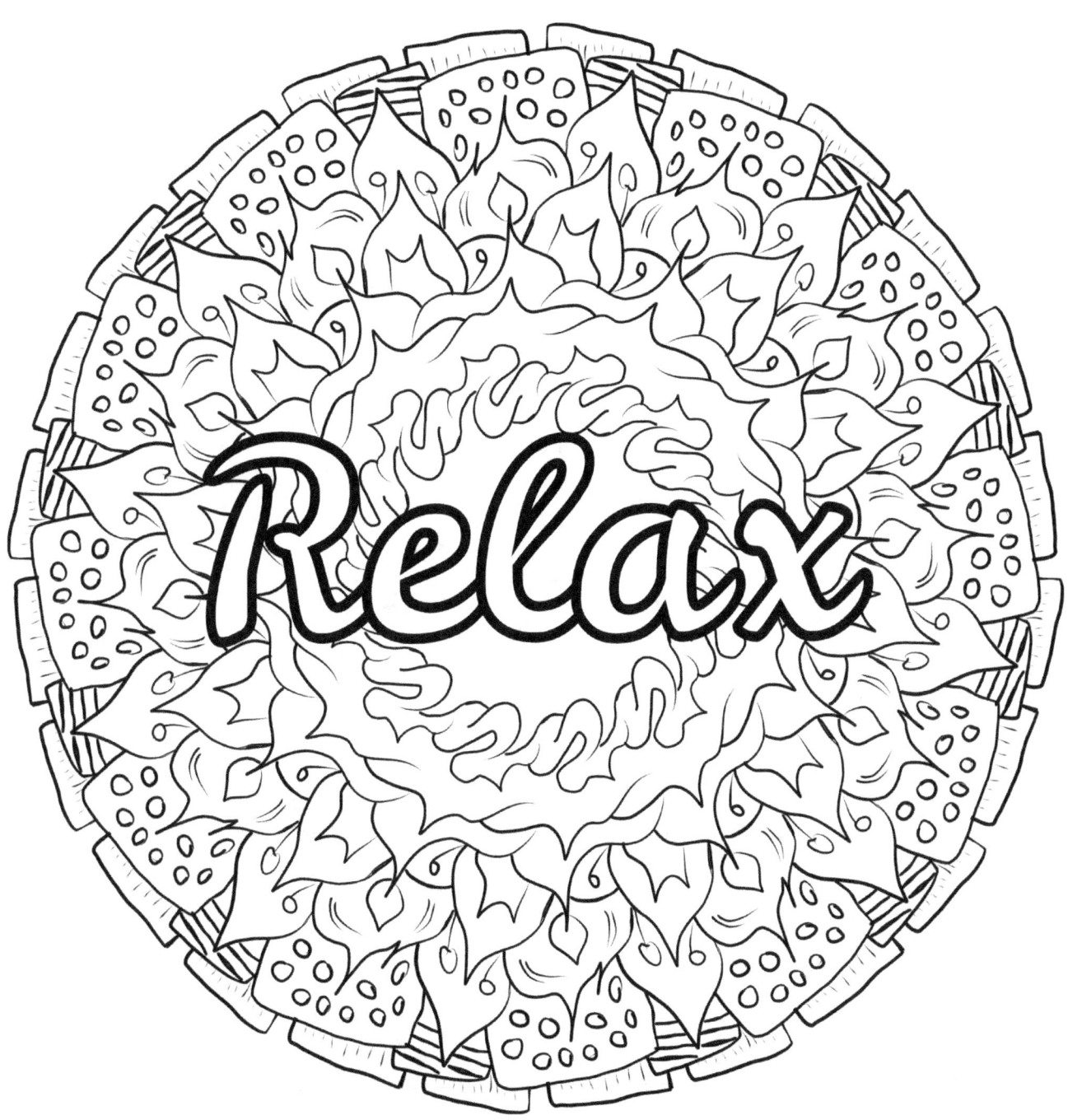

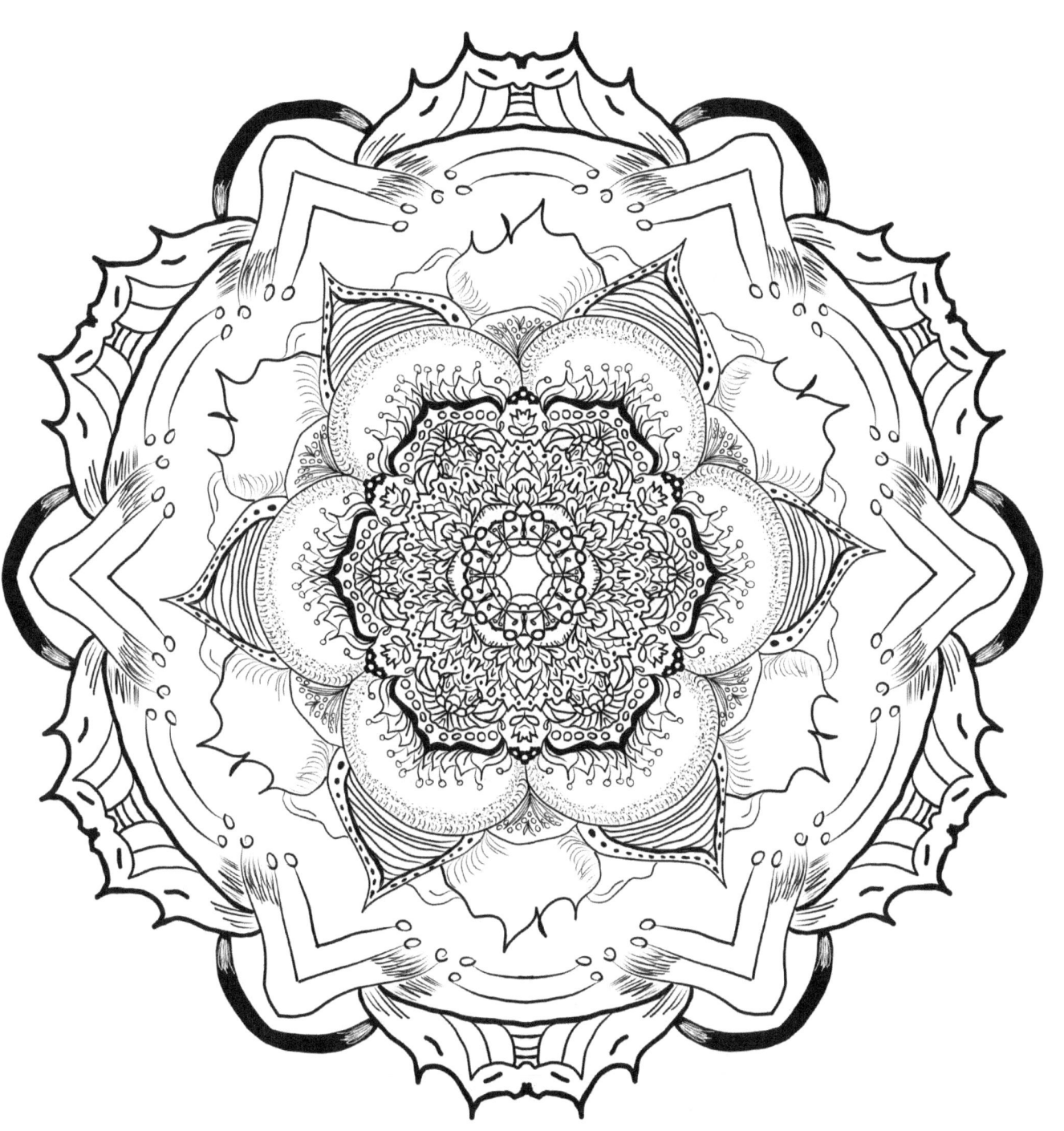

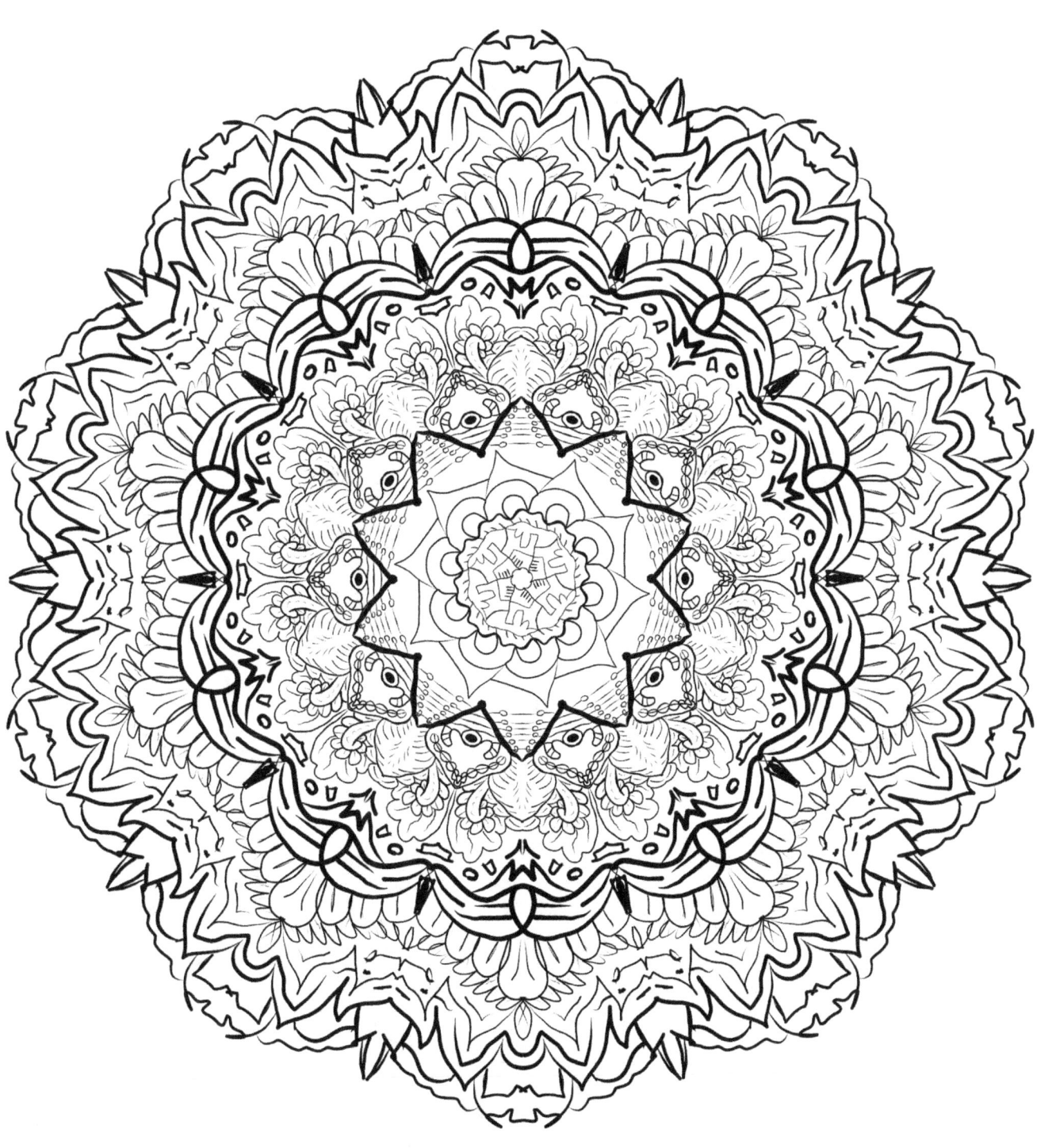

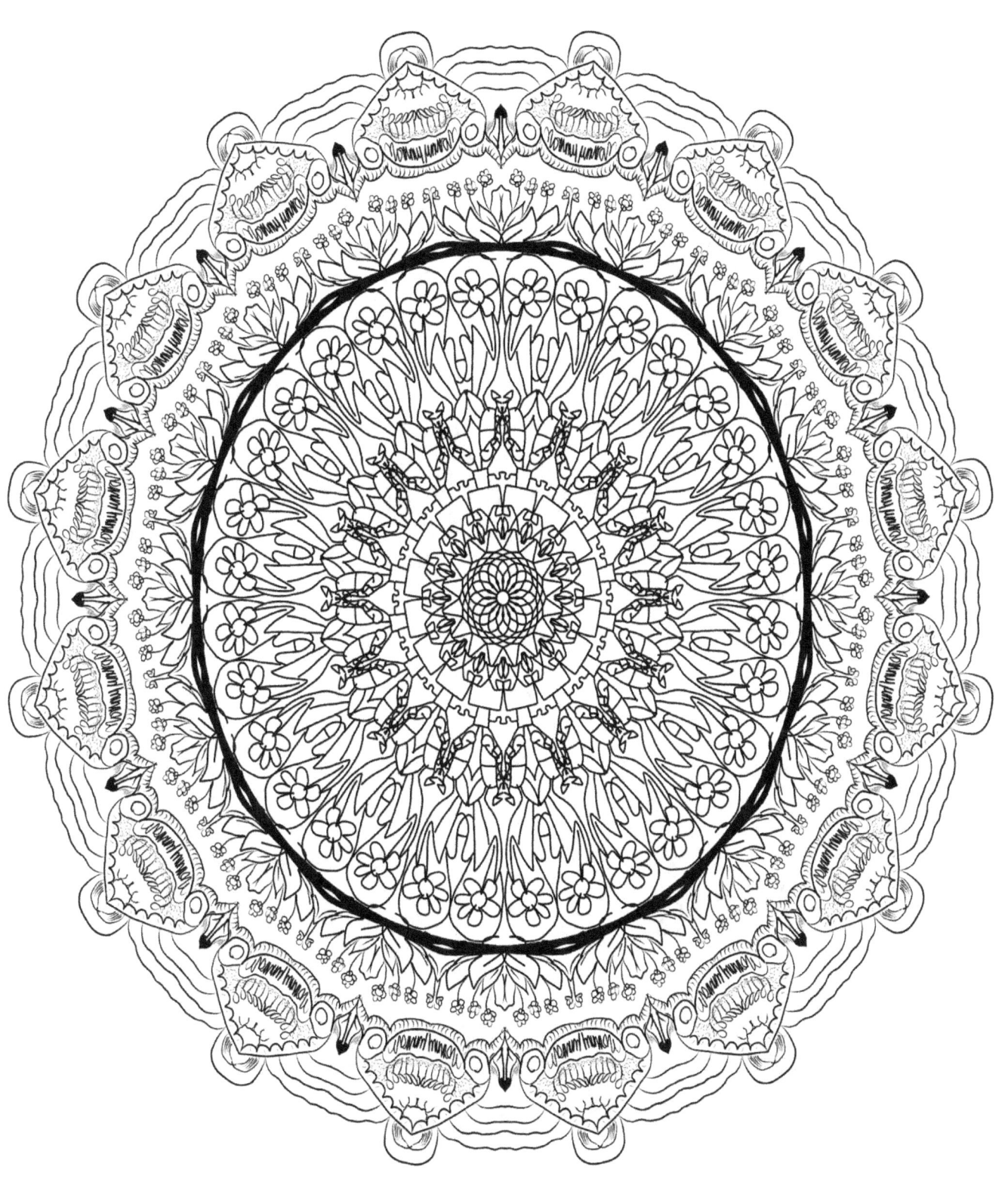

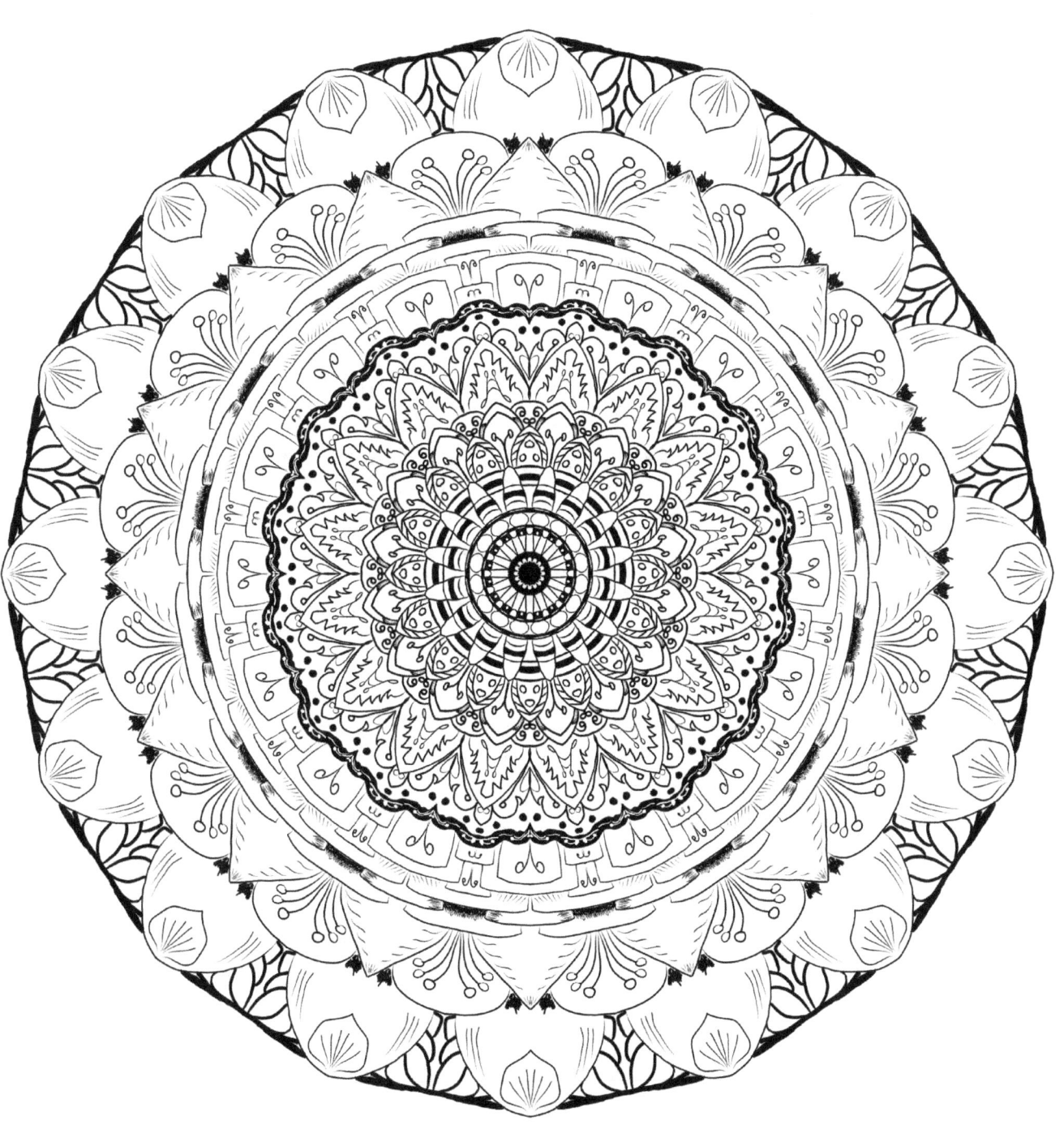

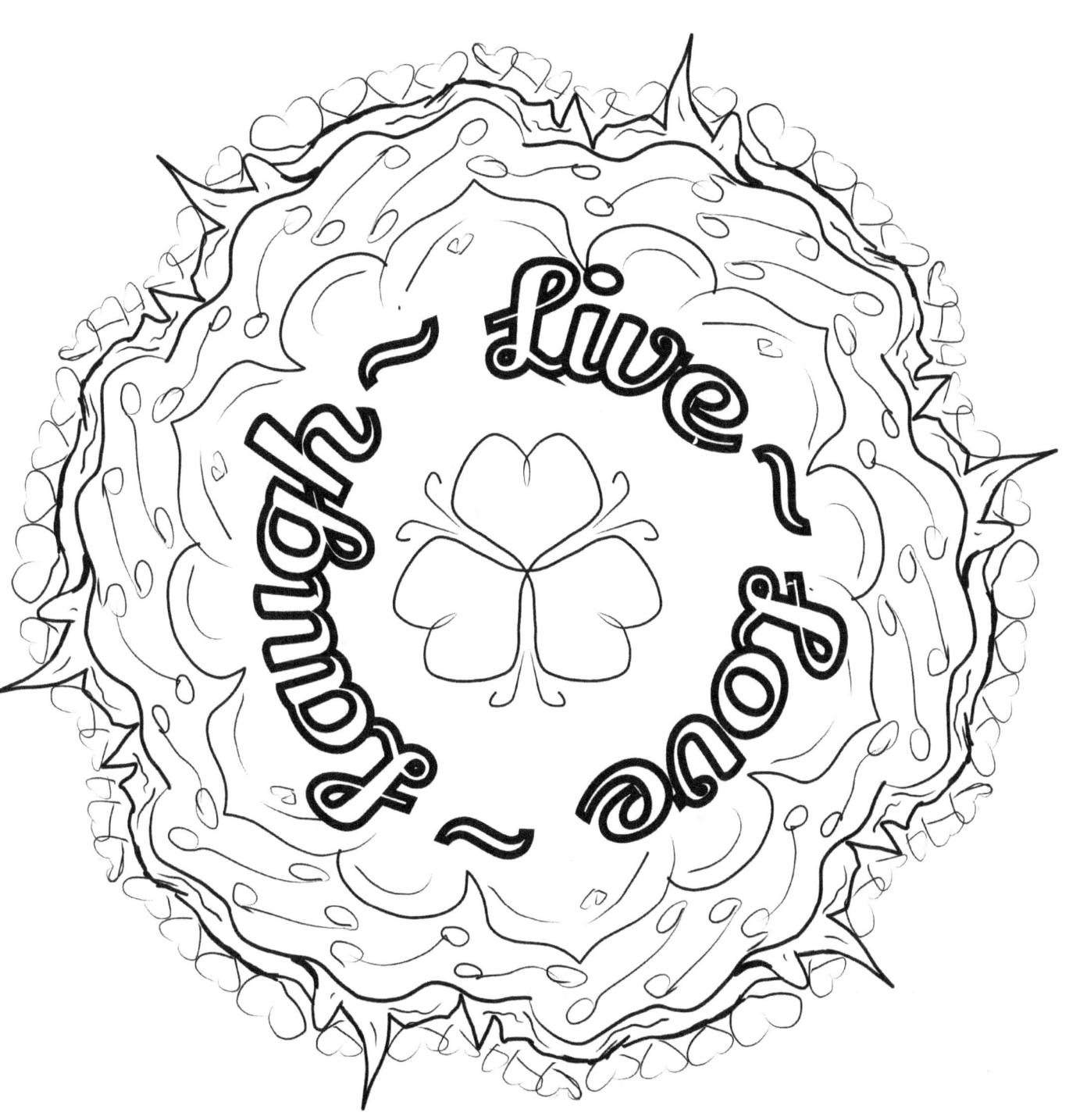

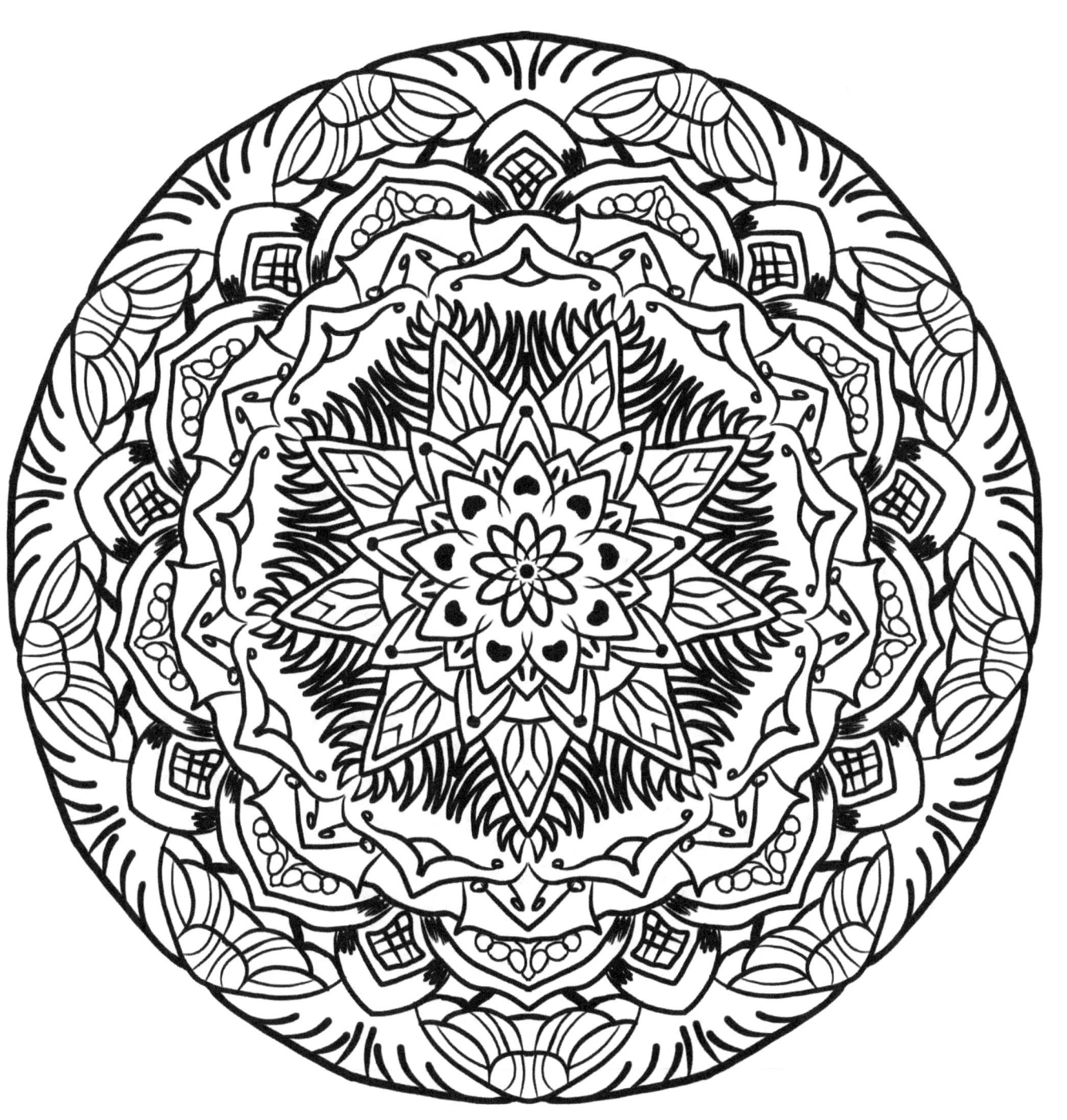

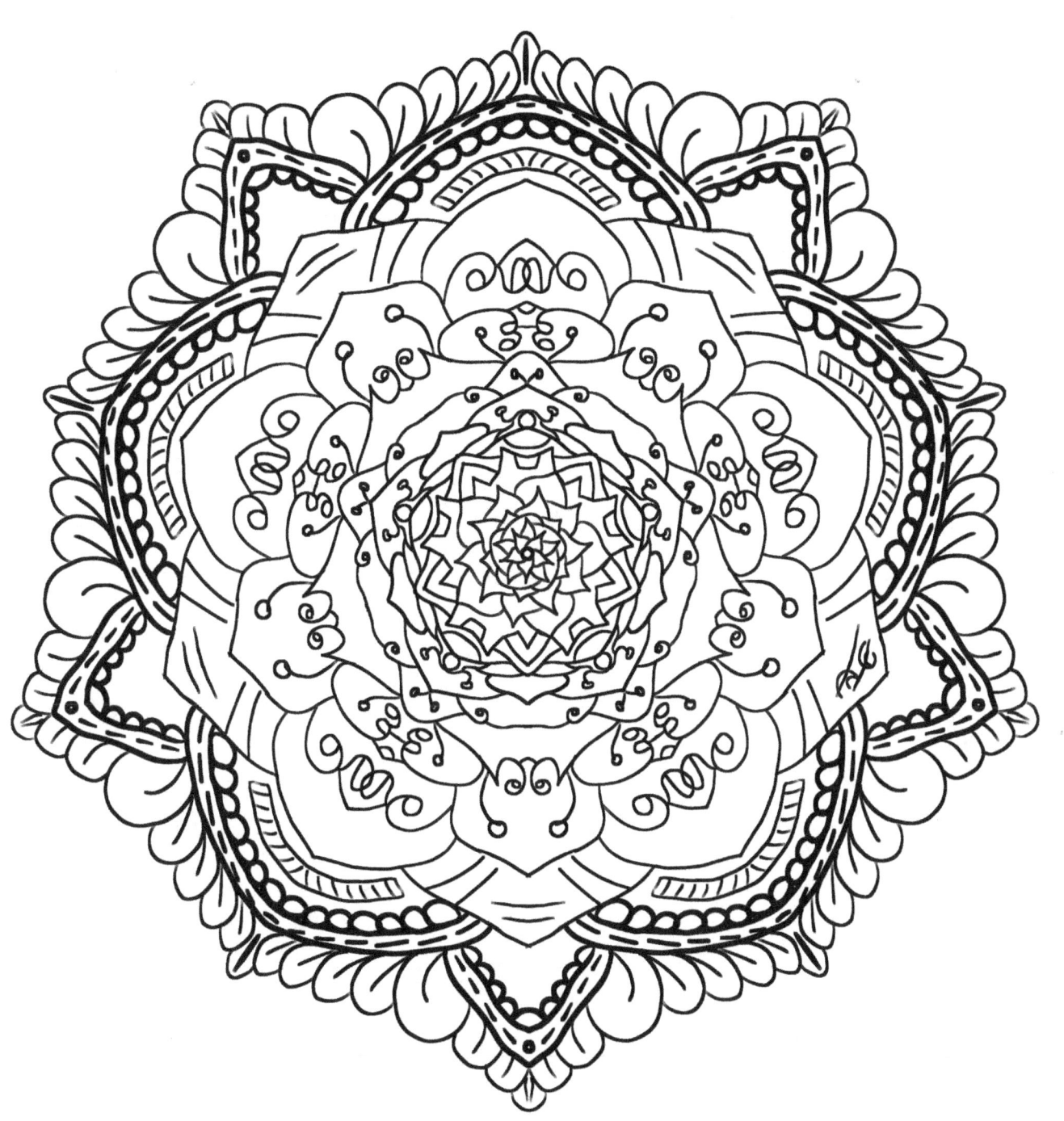

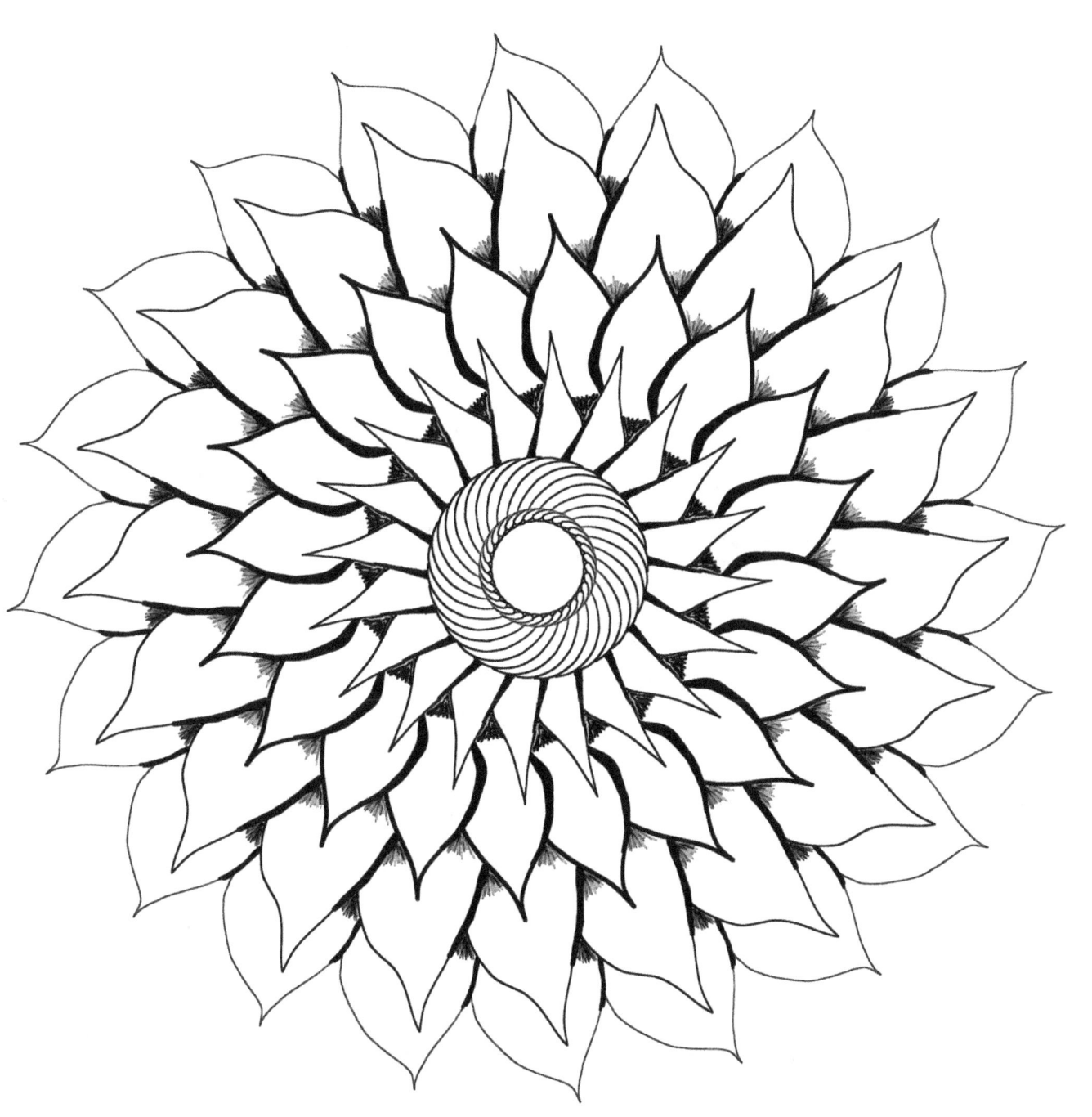